CW01466185

A JOHN CLARE FLORA

Trent Editions

Trent Editions aims to reproduce and republish landmark texts in handsome and accessible modern editions.

Trent Essays
Writers on the craft and context of writing

Series editor: John Goodridge (Emeritus Professor of English, Nottingham Trent University)

Jim Burns, *Beats, Bohemians and Intellectuals*, ed. **John Freeman** (2000)
Peter Porter, *Saving From the Wreck* (2001)
John Lucas, *Starting to Explain* (2003)
Ronald Blythe, *Talking About John Clare* (1999); *A Writer's Daybook* (2006)
Gregory Woods, *The Myth of the Last Taboo* (2016)

Our other series are:

American Recoveries
Key texts from the cultural memory of North America

Early Modern Writing (silver covers)
Recovering radical manuscript and printed texts from the cultural margins

Poetry Recoveries
Reconnecting poets to their own time and ours

Postcolonial Writings (maroon covers)
Radical voices of the colonial past, speaking to the postcolonial present

Radical Fictions
Radical novels and innovative fiction, with an emphasis on writers of the British Isles

Radical Recoveries
The history and development of working-class, radical and popular print culture

For further information please contact Trent Editions,
School of Arts and Humanities, Mary Ann Evans Building,
Nottingham Trent University, Clifton Lane,
Nottingham NG11 8NS, or use your
internet search engine to find our web page.

A John Clare Flora

M. M. Mahood

Foreword by Richard Mabey

Trent Editions

2016

Published by Trent Editions, 2016

Trent Editions
School of Arts and Humanities
Mary Ann Evans Building
Nottingham Trent University
Clifton Lane, Nottingham NG11 8NS

© This edition: M. M. Mahood 2016
The rights of the author have been asserted.

Designed and typeset by typesoflight

Printed by imprintdigital

ISBN: 978-1-84233-159-0

Front cover image: Pasqueflower, *Pulsatilla vulgaris*, still surviving at Barnack despite 'the plough that destroyer of wild flowers' having 'rooted it out of its long inherited dwelling'; see p. 36. Photo: Bridget R. Smith.

Contents

Acknowledgements

My thanks go first to Richard Mabey for his interest and encouragement when this book was no more than a stark list which I hoped I might be able to transform into a small sister of his splendid *Flora Britannica*. At that stage I had no first-hand knowledge of Clare's part of the country, so my first task was to discover how many of the flowers on my list could still be found there. Chris Gardiner, Natural England's Senior Reserves Manager in the area, and Jean Stowe, a committee member of the Langdyke Trust, both responded to my enquiries with invaluable species lists, and Jean also with her husband Iain's and her own skilful photographs; David Broughton, a Vice-county Recorder for the Botanical Society of Britain and Ireland, supplied me with up-to-the-minute information about the rarer flowers; Sheila Wells went out on my behalf and found some of them growing just where Clare said they did; from the start the late Peter Moyse shared with me his knowledge and appreciation of the landscape, trees and flowers of Clare's countryside. To all, my thanks.

Jean Stowe also put me in touch with the late Bridget Smith, whose combination of a lifelong pleasure in our native flora with a deep appreciation of Clare's poetry has been an inspiration to me ever since. Moreover, it was Bridget who prevailed on her former colleague in the Nature Conservancy Council, Philip Oswald, to scrutinise my draft manuscript. I am profoundly grateful to him for the scholarly accuracy and meticulous attention to detail that have saved me from a number of blunders (any that remain will be my oversights) and also for the zest with which he has provided titbits of botanical lore to liven up the more humdrum entries. Subsequently he took on the tasks of editing my text, compiling the index of plants and making the final selection of photographs from a substantially larger number that I should have liked to include. Other botanists who have generously and knowledgeably responded to my out-of-the-blue appeals for information are Clive Stace, Evelyn Stevens, Christopher Grey-Wilson and Andrea Wolfe.

Because my chief concern throughout this project has been with Clare the poet, I am especially grateful to Eric Robinson who – among other kindnesses – has allowed me to quote freely from his monumental Oxford English Texts edition of the poetry. I have addressed many queries about Clare's scientific friendships and his reading to Bob Heyes, whose unfailingly helpful replies have been rich in relevant detail; and when it came to viewing Clare in his wider social and literary setting, I have been especially privileged in having John Goodridge's input while preparing this volume. For information about Margaret Grainger, whose work on Clare as naturalist has not had the attention it deserves, I am indebted once again to Eric Robinson, and also to Paul Foster, Tim Chilcott and Simon Chandler. I am also grateful to Sam Ward for his input and for designing and typesetting the book.

I am most sincerely grateful to all those who supplied the beautiful photographs that adorn this book – Iain Stowe (IS), Philip Oswald (PHO), Jean Stowe (JS), Peter Moyse (PM), Bridget Smith (BRS), Peter Payne (PIP) and Barbro Jones (BJ).

Abbreviations

agg. aggregate

By Himself *John Clare: By Himself*, ed. Eric Robinson and David Powell (Ashington and Manchester: Mid-Northumberland Arts Group and Carcanet Press, 1996)

Druce George Claridge Druce, *The Flora of Northamptonshire* (Arbroath: T. Buncle, 1930)

EP *The Early Poems of John Clare 1804–1822*, ed. Eric Robinson and David Powell, associate ed. Margaret Grainger (Oxford: Clarendon Press, 1989), two volumes

GW2 Gill Gent and Rob Wilson, *The Flora of Northamptonshire and the Soke of Peterborough* (Rothwell: Robert Wilson Designs, 2013)

Grigson Geoffrey Grigson, *The Englishman's Flora* (London: Phoenix House, 1975)

Letters *The Letters of John Clare*, ed. Mark Storey (Oxford: Clarendon Press, 1985)

LP *The Later Poems of John Clare 1837–1864*, ed. Eric Robinson and David Powell, associate ed. Margaret Grainger (Oxford: Clarendon Press, 1984), two volumes, pagination throughout

Mabey Richard Mabey, supported by Common Ground, *Flora Britannica* (London: Sinclair-Stevenson, 1996)

MP   John Clare, *Poems of the Middle Period 1822–1837*, ed. Eric Robinson, David Powell, and P. M. S. Dawson (Oxford: Clarendon Press), volumes I–II, 1996; volumes III–IV, 1998; volume V, 2003, five volumes in all

NH   *The Natural History Prose Writings of John Clare*, ed. Margaret Grainger (Oxford: Clarendon Press, 1983)

sp.   species (singular)

spp.   species (plural)

ssp.   subspecies

SSSI   Site of Special Scientific Interest

var.   variety

Wells   Terry C. E. Wells, *The Flora of Huntingdonshire and the Soke of Peterborough* (Upwood, Huntingdon: Huntingdonshire Fauna and Flora Society and T. C. E. Wells, 2003)

List of Illustrations

Plates are between pages 92 and 93.

Foreword

Molly Mahood's *The Poet as Botanist* (2008) is one of the seminal books on 'the relationship between biological thought and the poetic process'. Its lightly-worn scholarship and mischievous humour perfectly express her theme that the best of poetry is a kind of science, truth forged out of a marriage between incisive observation and imaginative insight. John Clare is in many ways the hero of the book, and Molly quotes the poignant self-description he had inscribed on the back of his portrait – 'Bard of the wild flowers / Rain-washed and wind-shaken'. It's a declaration of solidarity with these other commoners, and a sentiment that will be felt in the bone by every worker in the field, scientific or poetic.

Clare was hostile to the Latinate reductions of Linnaean botany, which he called 'the Dark System'. Yet he could not have stopped being an acute botanical observer if he tried. His verse on Lesser Celandine identifies the flower as decisively as any field-guide: 'Reflecting on its leaves the suns bright rays / That sets its pointed glories in a blaze'. Combing not just his verse but his journals and letters, Molly has found that Clare knew and noted more than 400 plant species, and it is these references that she has collected together in this remarkable volume, *A John Clare Flora*, which somehow contrives to be both magisterial and intimate. It ranges from scarce orchids which Clare differentiated by their addresses, to emblematic weeds: 'To an Insignificant Flower Obscurely Blooming in a Lonely Wild'.

Clare's impulse, which joins him with the field botanist, was to write his impressions 'down on the spot'. 'It is a way of working', Molly comments, 'that makes him the most transparent of poets: a finder, not a maker. It means that for him there is no fallow period followed by a recollection in tranquillity that will enable him to shape his reflections into an artefact.' There is surely no more spontaneous, cross-species hug in English poetry than 'Welcome old Maytey', the opening lines of 'To an April Daisy'. Yet if there was no period of tranquil reflection, these moments of immediacy and communion were informed by Clare's reading, and his understanding of the society he so vulnerably inhabited. In his startling and precocious poem, 'Shadows of Taste', Clare prefigures ecology by suggesting that 'taste' is a faculty enjoyed by all living things, as their instinctive choice of – and comfortableness in – their own habitats. In humans he sees it as the conscious appreciation of wild things in their 'cultural' habitats. To add context is Molly's special contribution in *A John Clare Flora*, as she relates Clare's passionate, particular celebrations of plants to the literature and science and agricultural turmoil that were swimming about his head as he "dropped down" to engage with his vegetal companions.

The *Flora* has, at times, the melancholy air of an elegy, as a picture of a countryside of almost unimaginable floral richness emerges only to be destroyed as Clare watches. But it is also a manifesto. Helpston villagers had a tradition of studding pieces of turf with wild flowers and mounting them on their doors. The results were called Midsummer Cushions (a tag Clare used for as the title of one of his poetry collections). Molly's *Flora* is a John Clare Cushion, a loving collection of his poetic flowers, rooted in the native culture that fostered them, and an implicit plea for their continuance.

Richard Mabey

Introduction

Seeds of some plants can remain dormant for many years, centuries even, until the right conditions of soil and climate make it possible for them to germinate. So it has been with this book, the seed of which may be said to have been sown on 11 March 1825 by Joseph Henderson, head gardener of Milton Hall near Peterborough, in a letter to his poet friend John Clare who lived in nearby Helpston.

'With respect to the Flora of this neighbourhood', Henderson wrote,

> I cannot satisfy myself as to any plan, except the old one of Notes on the plants mentioned in your works, a mere catalogue of the plants found in the neighbourhood might easily be made out, but that would neither meet your views nor mine. If you were to take as the subject and title of a poem The Poets Flower Garden you would lay the best foundation for the Scheme. The woods and the fields, where Nature is Gardener, would furnish your materials and in it you might embody all the local names you are acquainted with and when we make our long talked of excursion I shall perhaps be able to help you to others. ... On these and the plants mentioned in your works generally I would write Notes, giving the Botanical name and any other remark that might be thought interesting, which with our own observations might follow on as an appendix to your works.

It is evident from this that at some time Clare and Henderson had had thoughts of collaborating in a commentary on the many allusions to flowers and trees in Clare's poetry (indeed a letter written two years previously by Henderson hints at this), but that Clare had since come up with another suggestion. As luck would have it, his side of the correspondence has not survived except for a few notes written after he moved to another village in 1832. But an entry made the previous autumn in the journal that he was keeping at this period records his resolve to write a book, to be called 'A Garden of Wild Flowers', on the model of a recently published guide to pot plants, Elizabeth Kent's *Flora Domestica*. Clare's book was to be embellished 'with quotations from poets and others', as hers had been, but it is clear that what he had in mind was a practical and informative prose work. He had begun to realise that the reading public's interest in poetry, intense as it had been for the past quarter-century, was now in steep decline – as the fate of his own publications illustrates. Compared with the phenomenal success of *Poems Descriptive of Rural Life and Scenery*, published by the firm of Taylor and Hessey in 1820, sales of *The Village Minstrel* in 1821 had been slow, and its 'second' edition, a copy of which he had given Henderson, was made up from unbound sheets of the first. Nor in 1825 was John Taylor, now on his own, in any hurry to bring out a third collection. A further two and a half years would pass before *The Shepherd's Calendar* was published – and widely ignored – while out of the great body of verse Clare wrote in his thirties only a thin and somewhat unrepresentative selection appeared in 1835, under a different imprint, as *The Rural Muse*.

Poetry was the breath of life to Clare and he would go on writing it almost to the end of his days. But in the 1820s prose must have appeared to offer the surer means of feeding his family. In consequence, during the time he was engaged on the series of descriptive and narrative poems suggested by Taylor as the ground-plan of *The Shepherd's Calendar*, he embarked on a book about birds (in epistolary form) which grew, by the addition of material on flowers and animals, into the beginnings of a Natural History of Helpston. So however flattered he may have felt on 11 March 1825 by Henderson's casual mention of his 'works', his journal entry of the same date makes no reference to the plan to which his friend so firmly adhered. Rather it hints at a determination to guard his right to describe the wild life of his area in his own way: 'Intend to call my Natural History of Helpstone Biographys of Birds and Flowers'.

Henderson's idea, it would seem, had fallen onto ground that was not ready to receive it. But his plan to bring together into a whole Clare's many evocations of the green life that burgeoned and blossomed all round him has long seemed to me too good to have been abandoned. Accordingly I have taken the whole range of Clare's allusions to plants in his verse and prose as the basis of the present work, which is in the form and order of a wild-flower guide. My hope is that it will confirm admirers of Clare's poetry in their belief that in his writings no less than in his garden he was, as village tradition maintained, 'a wonderful man with flowers'; and that naturalists and environmentalists may find here a faithful picture of the plant life, both native and introduced, of one small area of the English Midlands as it was before twentieth-century farming practices transformed much of it into prairie-like monoculture.

On any map of the Midlands printed before 1965, the County of Northamptonshire has roughly the shape of a game bird on the ground. Its back forms part of the line of limestone uplands that stretches south-west to north-east across lowland England. Northampton, the county town in whose General Lunatic Asylum John Clare passed, or let pass, the last third of his life until his death in 1864, lies in its belly. Its head, craned forward due east into the Fens, is the area still known by its medieval name of the Soke of Peterborough, and its eye – very suitably – is the village of Helpston, where Clare was born in 1793. The resemblance, however, was destroyed in 1965, when the bird was decapitated: the Soke was removed from Northamptonshire's administrative control and attached to Huntingdonshire, prior to both areas being absorbed ten years later into the County of Cambridgeshire. Fortunately for my purpose, the Botanical Society of Britain and Ireland continues to use the former boundaries of Northamptonshire, designated Vice-county 32, for its records and maps.

Conforming, perhaps, a little to his publisher's wish to present him as a prodigy from a rural limbo, Clare described his birthplace as 'a gloomy village … on the brink of the Lincolnshire fens'. But as one of his London friends pointed out, he must have had something better than 'fenny flats' about him – 'or else where do all the fine things come from that get into your verse?' The answer is that they came, by and large, from the tracts of open grassland that lay to the west and south of Helpston: grazing commons of which the vestiges are even today home to four times more species of wild flowers than is the low-lying area that begins in the immediate neighbourhood of Helpston and includes the village of Northborough to which Clare flitted in 1832. On that level terrain and within six or so miles north and east of his birthplace, there had once stretched 'the Moors' that gave their name to his most famous protest poem: 800 acres of summer pasture that in his boyhood had been the haunt of marsh-orchids but that had recently been enclosed, drained and put under the plough. The result of these changes was that, with the exception of some species-rich wetland across which the five shallow arches of Lolham Briggs carried the Roman road known as King Street, there were very few areas north or east of Helpston where it was possible for the adult Clare to look for flowers. As a result his instinct when, in his own words, he 'went to wander with the double intention of rhyming and seeking wild plants', was to head west or south to the upland commons that were still in large part unenclosed.

A special feature of that limestone landscape was its scattering of disused and overgrown workings which, according to John Morton's *Natural History of Northamptonshire* (1712), afforded 'a Noble Variety of Rare Plants, and will give the best Entertainment to a Botanist': words that anticipate Clare's definition of happiness as freedom 'to wander among the hills and hollows of heaths which have been old stone quarries'. Some of his best finds were in the most famous of these abandoned quarries, Barnack Hills and Holes, which lies within easy walking distance of Helpston. Six hundred years previously, the site had yielded up massive blocks of ragstone for the building of Peterborough Cathedral. Abandoned at the beginning of the sixteenth century, it had, by Clare's day, been transformed by natural processes into a haven for wild flowers and this has resulted in our own time in its being declared a National Nature Reserve. Only a few miles further to the south-west it has a sylvan counterpart in a relic of the medieval Rockingham Forest, known as the Bedford Purlieus, which retains what some botanists believe to be the richest woodland flora in England. Clare, it would seem, never got quite so far in his wanderings, but many smaller fragments of flower-filled ancient woodland were within his reach in this gently undulating countryside. So too was what in his time was Northamptonshire's finest hunting-ground for marsh-orchids and other wetland plants, Sutton Bog, a small surviving part of which is today protected as a nature reserve.

In the days before Clare became a published poet and was still a young labourer with some training in gardening skills, his flower-seeking was largely undertaken in search of plants for his own and his friends' gardens.

Very little is known about these friends other than his near neighbour John Billings, but the scraps of information we have about the rest suggest that several of them were connected in one way or another with the retinues of the big houses – Ufford Hall, Bainton House, Walcot Hall – that lie to the west of Helpston. Before his marriage in 1820 Clare spent his Sundays in the company of one of these friends, Thomas Porter of Ashton, and together they roamed woods and pastures in search of uncommon flowers. Once found, these had to be identified from books, since village people could put very few names to local plants. Seventeenth-century works such as Thomas Johnson's revision of Gerard's *Herbal* and John Parkinson's *Theatrum Botanicum*, whether inherited by his friends or picked up at fairs, were the first sources of nomenclature for Clare, who was ill-at-ease with the binomial Latin names and Latinate terminology of recent floras arranged according to Linnaeus's classification. He and his friends also appear to have made many of their identifications out of practical guides to gardening which, on the assumption that readers would transplant native flowers into their gardens, drew little or no distinction between wild and cultivated plants.

1820 was also the year in which the double excitement of becoming a published poet and of visiting London for the first time raised Clare's hopes to their highest point. By late 1821 however he was beginning to dread being thrust back into the limitations of a casual labourer's daily life. A piece of good fortune that freed him, at least temporarily, from these fears was that around this time he made the acquaintance of two senior employees of Milton Hall near Peterborough, which was the summer residence of the Fitzwilliam family. Milton's house steward, Edmund Artis, a keen naturalist who was diverted to a lifetime of archaeology through his fortuitous discovery of Roman remains in the neighbourhood, appears to have been the first to befriend Clare. But his more lasting and fruitful friendship was to be with Lord Milton's head gardener, Joseph Henderson.

Like many of those who looked after the pleasure grounds, hothouses and kitchen gardens of the English aristocracy, Henderson was a well-educated Scot who regarded horticulture as a serious calling. Already a capable botanist (he would one day be made an associate member of the

Linnean Society), he was able by his interest and knowledgeability to inject new life into Clare's flower-hunting. Seventy of his letters to Clare are extant, and the early ones show us how quickly their friendship ripened. A first formal note in the third person, probably written in the early spring of 1822, is followed on 22 April by one that ends 'I am, Dear Friend Yours very sincerely' and, a few weeks later, by an invitation to join Henderson, Artis and others 'on a sort of Plant-hunting, Butterfly-catching expedition' to Whittlesea Mere in Huntingdonshire. It is unlikely that Clare was back from his second visit to London in time to take part in this outing; and there were other occasions when the friends' attempts to plant-hunt together were foiled, though it was more often Henderson who was obliged to cry off on account of his duties at Milton. But plants, both wild and cultivated, are a frequent theme of letters that were as often as not accompanied by seeds, cuttings or offshoots from the Milton nurseries, while Clare's gratitude for such gifts might take the tangible form of a bundle of native orchids for his friend's collection.

It was probably in the course of these exchanges that Henderson discovered Clare's fierce prejudice against Linnaeus's 'dark system' and set about countering it with gentle persistence, at one time arguing its usefulness at length in a letter and at another inviting Clare to join him at Milton for 'a day or two of very interesting work' over the thirty-six illustrated volumes of Sowerby's *English Botany* (1790–1814). A year or two later he spent hours compiling – mostly from Sir James Smith's text to Sowerby but with careful updating – a guide to wild orchids that would aid and encourage Clare in his quest for the rarer species. Eventually, it would seem, he won over his friend: Clare acquired Smith's handy *Compendium of the British Flora* (1829) and jotted down the titles of similar works. A heightened and informed awareness of the green life round him is one of the things that makes Clare's poems of the 1830s, as they were assembled by him into *The Midsummer Cushion*, his finest collection, and in this Henderson's intimate understanding of plants most certainly played its part.

Moreover, this was only a small part of all he did for his friend. A well-read man with a love of poetry, he was able to offer positive criticism of Clare's drafts and even lend a hand in improving the wording of a passage.

More importantly, he responded with sensitivity to Clare's attacks of profound depression, countering them by sensible advice on how he might maintain his physical health and with repeated invitations to share the good company – and by implication the much-needed good food – to be had at Milton. He also helped him sort out his financial affairs and, once it became clear that Clare's family could not hope to live on the income from his writings, he used his influence with Lord Milton to obtain for him the offer of a roomy cottage with a smallholding at Northborough on the edge of the Fens. It was through no fault of Henderson's that this move of under three miles proved disastrous. Put by reason of increasing debility beyond reach of his beloved woods and heaths, Clare became more and more alienated until in 1837 it became necessary for him to be admitted, on John Taylor's initiative, to a private asylum in Epping Forest. From there he would, in 1841, make his penniless way home on foot, only to be immured some months later in Northampton's recently-built asylum.

Henderson's name occurs many times in the pages that follow, as do two others: Druce and Grainger. George Claridge Druce (1850–1932), himself a Northamptonshire man born and bred, was able to recall once catching a glimpse of Clare in Northampton – 'a little, pathetic distraught figure gazing into the sky'. A pharmacist by profession but a botanist by vocation, he was the first to recognise the extent of the poet's knowledge. Within eight years of Clare's death he began work on what became *The Flora of Northamptonshire ... with short biographical notices of the botanists who have contributed to Northamptonshire botany during the last three centuries*. In Clare's case, the 'short notice' is expanded to many pages of an Introduction that quotes, from those of his poems that were then in print, allusions to 135 flowers and trees, of which over forty are distinguished in the main text as 'first records' for the county.

Much of Druce's field work on his *Flora* was completed by 1879 when he bought a pharmacy in Oxford's High Street (he was to figure in *Zuleika Dobson*) and turned his attention to the plant life of the South Midland counties. The result of this was that when the Northamptonshire Flora was finally published as a whole in 1930 the overall picture it gave was of the county's vegetation as it had been in mid-Victorian times. For the Soke, however, many of its records are of more recent date because Druce, especially after his retirement in 1905, repeatedly refreshed his botanical knowledge of Clare's countryside by visits to his friend Charles Rothschild, the banker, naturalist and campaigner for nature reserves, whose country home was close to the Soke border. Sometimes an isolated exclamation mark, a botanist's shorthand for 'I've seen this with my own eyes', suggests a fresh search had been made with Clare in mind. The question, for example, of whether Clare's 'wild stalking canterbury bell' can have been the Giant Bellflower appears to be settled by the absence of all reference to Clare or Helpston under *Campanula latifolia* and the entry 'Helpstone, *Clare.* !' under '*C. Trachelium* L. Nettle-leaved Bellflower'.

Impressive as is Druce's reliance on Clare in *The Flora of Northamptonshire*, a glance through the following pages will reveal that in fact Clare knew and was able to name three times the number of plants with which Druce credits him. The reason for this discrepancy is that in 1930 only a quarter of Clare's surviving verse was in print and his prose writings were virtually unknown. The following year, however, Edmund Blunden produced a volume of Clare's autobiographical writings, and the appearance in 1951 of John and Anne Tibble's *The Prose of John Clare* prompted another leading botanist, F. H. Perring, to draw on it for additions to Druce's list. But it was not until the second half of last century that our access to Clare as a writer of both verse and prose was transformed as completely as was, in the same period, the countryside he knew. On the ground, the flowers he loved dwindled in their numbers year by year and sometimes vanished entirely before the onslaught of intensive farming. In the world of publishing, however, the corpus of Clare's writings grew and grew. Margaret Grainger's edition of *The Natural History Prose Writings of John Clare*, a work that has been all-important for my undertaking, was published in 1983, to be followed two years later by Mark Storey's *The Letters of John Clare*. Crowning all was the completion, by Eric Robinson and his fellow editors, of the Oxford English Texts edition of Clare's poetry in nine volumes (1984–2003) containing over three thousand poems, the great majority from autograph manuscripts. All in all, these years produced a wealth of writings that has rescued Clare from the dubious reputation of the Peasant Poet and set him among the foremost Romantics.

It has also made possible the compilation of *A John Clare Flora*. While working on this compilation I have felt special indebtedness to Margaret Grainger (1936–1992), who was born and grew up in Stamford, a few miles west of Helpston. Familiarity with the John Clare Collection of manuscripts in the Peterborough Museum, of which she produced a descriptive catalogue in 1973, as well as with those in the Northampton Public Library, put her in an ideal position to assemble all the poet's natural history observations. A further advantage was that she was a born naturalist who succeeded, for example, in finding almost all the orchids mentioned by Clare that were still extant in the area. She also had the good fortune to be helped in her undertaking by her fellow-townsman John H. Chandler, who was a skilled and experienced botanist.

Not only does my own botanical knowledge fall short of Grainger's and Chandler's, but I lack their lifelong familiarity with Clare country. Consequently there are very few places in this book where I have ventured to question their identification of this or that plant. Where I have done so, it has been with the backing of one or both of two modern works that cover the area: *The Flora of Northamptonshire and the Soke of Peterborough* by Gill Gent and Rob Wilson, first published in 1995, and Terry C. E. Wells's *The Flora of Huntingdonshire and the Soke of Peterborough* (2006). Because of the greater precision of its distribution maps the latter, to which John Chandler made substantial contributions, was the more useful to me when I started to collect Clare's allusions. But the balance was righted at the end of 2012 by the publication of a completely revised second edition of the Gent and Wilson flora which now conforms with current practice by mapping the distribution of each species in a grid of 2 × 2 kilometre squares. Regrettably, though, neither flora makes use of Grainger's rich assemblage of Clare's notes and records, many of which tell us exactly where he found this or that plant.

Because the 1995 *Flora of Northamptonshire* is in some respects an update, using modern recording techniques, of Druce's Flora of the county, it was possible for Duncan McCollin, Linda Moore and Tim Sparks to take it as the basis for a detailed study of changes in the area's floral diversity. Their findings, published in *Biological Conservation* 90 (2000), show that by that date a hundred species recorded by Druce had vanished from within Northamptonshire's one-time boundaries, while the frequency of many others had sharply declined. In the belief that readers will share my concern over the decline or disappearance of so many wild flowers known to Clare, I have drawn attention to many of these losses, which reflect the highest recorded rates of extinctions for any British county.

It is some relief to learn from the second edition of Gent and Wilson that there are signs of the overall decline slowing down, thanks to both worthy and less worthy factors that range from scientifically-planned habitat renewal, through light-hearted dispersal from wild-flower seed packets, to a general neglect of woodland that is all to the benefit of shade-loving species. But, outside nature reserves, the profusion and the diversity that gave such seasonal joy to Clare and his contemporaries have indubitably gone for ever. Meanwhile, disappearances and occasional rediscoveries of individual species continue, and I have tried to bring the story up to the date of publication by consulting those who are currently recording the flora of the Helpston area for the Botanical Society of Britain and Ireland and for various environmental bodies. Their ready and generous help is acknowledged on an earlier page.

Flowers spelt home to Clare, and my record of the plants that he knew contains very few that he met for the first time outside the Soke. When he was employed a few miles north of Stamford in the years 1817 to 1820, he was struck by the beauty of the Rutland landscape; but its flora would have appeared to him to be much the same as that of the countryside to the south of Helpston. Vivid as were his memories of the wild Lilies-of-the-valley that he gathered for Martha Turner – soon to be his wife, Patty – from a wood close to her home near Casterton, these enchanting flowers grew and are said still to grow near his birthplace. Nor did his four homesick years among the towering beeches and hornbeams of Epping Forest increase the tally beyond a species or two, for the poetry he was then writing reverts time and again to the small woods round Helpston. Again, flowers run riot through the lyrics of his last years, but though he may give some of them more generally known names than those they had in his earlier poems, as often as not he visualises them in a Helpston setting. The exceptions to this are for the most part nurserymen's introductions.

Northampton's authorities were proud of their General Asylum and saw to it that its grounds were well planted.

Cultivated flowers, shrubs and trees in fact account for about a quarter of the entries in my list. Nineteenth-century floras tended to exclude all such recent introductions, but the last century saw a growing realisation on the part of botanists that alien species which had integrated to the extent of naturalising in the countryside deserved to be given citizenship. Clive Stace's 1991 *New Flora of the British Isles* which, following the example of Richard Mabey in his *Flora Britannica* (1996), I took as my guide when I began to record Clare's flowers, includes all the plants that can be found in the wild in these islands, regardless of whether or not their forebears were brought here in comparatively recent times. It has been interesting to discover that only half a dozen of the numerous species that Clare knew as garden flowers have failed to show up somewhere in a 'wild' setting, and consequently do not qualify to appear in Stace's pages. I have given room to these few exotics, along with other aliens. But on reflection I have left out the many garden varieties of which Clare from time to time jotted down the names and which Grainger includes in her appendix of 'Plant Lists'. Though these memoranda are of interest in that they hint at the possibility that Clare hoped at one time to grow for profit what were then known as 'florists' flowers', he must have copied many of the names from catalogues without ever having set eyes on the plants themselves, while they for the most part were ephemeral cultivars of which only the names survive today.

There have been minor problems of what to include and what to exclude. Unsurprisingly, the lign-aloes of Clare's biblical paraphrases will not be found here, nor will his heavenly amaranths. I have however included, in the form of a brief Proem, his allusions to non-vascular plants – the ones that are too 'primitive' to stand up for themselves. It is true that these do not figure in conventional floras but in the early nineteenth century they were stirring up considerable interest among botanists; Henderson, for example, made what he calls a 'book' from a hundred dried species of moss that he collected locally. I have also given entries to the few species that Clare knew but could not put a name to, such as the 'tiny snow-white blossoms' on top of limestone walls in April, which, as the result of an appeal to other John Clare Society members, are here identified as Common Whitlowgrass, *Erophila verna*. Also included, because they played an important part in his life as a gardener, are plants that were given him by Henderson and other friends, even when no allusions of his own to them are to be found. All such in-or-out decisions are of course debatable, a fact that makes me reluctant to state an exact total number for all the plants in Clare's writings. It is safe, however, to say that he knew, and could put a name to, well over 400 species representative, by my count, of 282 genera.

This total is impressive enough to raise speculation about plants he does *not* name. Why, for example, is *Amaranthus caudatus*, a non-heavenly (some might say infernal) amaranth introduced from South America, the sole representative in his writings of the huge Goosefoot family? Is the reason that the tiny green flowers of many native species earn little notice from anybody? Or is it that the name Love-lies-bleeding has both an associative and a prosodic appeal not to be found in Fat-hen or orache? To me, Clare's most puzzling omission is the genus *Hypericum* – the beautiful and fascinating St John's-worts, several species of which are still common in the Soke. But, as he himself points out, it is easier to put names to those flowers whose first appearances constitute a calendar of spring than it is to distinguish between the great mass of summer blooms, many of which had at that place and time no local names.

Because even so modest a volume as this one is designed in the hope that readers will find it useful as a work of reference, the order in which to arrange its entries has cost me some anxious thought. Clare's journal entry about 'A Garden of Wild Flowers' implies that he would have preferred a commentary on his flowers to follow the simple alphabetical order used at the time by Elizabeth Kent and other authors of popular gardening works, rather than the Linnaean arrangement with its baggage of what he called unutterable words. Not that he would have been any happier with the 'natural' taxonomic system that, in Britain, was belatedly beginning to replace the artificial one of Linnaeus. For one thing, it demanded the use of many more Latinisms. Nonetheless the reordering of plant genera into families according to their observable affinities and the grouping of those families in a way that was held to demonstrate the Creator's supreme inventiveness had immediate appeal to the Victorians. At the same time, it helped to prepare the ground for the theory of evolution, in which affinities were replaced by actual relationships; theological questions aside, it was not difficult to substitute, for the image of all the species of vegetation constituting a great meadow in which like bloomed in proximity to like, the image of a tree-of-life putting out fresh growth through the whole of post-Cambrian time. This meant that right up to the closing decades of the last century there was still general confidence in the reliability of a botanical arrangement based on features visible to eye or microscope, and the most comprehensive of these, that of Arthur Cronquist, was used in its linear form by Stace in his *New Flora of the British Isles*, first published in 1991 and soon accepted as the standard British flora.

By that date however biologists, using new laboratory techniques, had begun to explore plant DNA in quest of links at the molecular level; and while many of their results gave reassuring support to long-recognised family groupings, others revealed quite unexpected relationships and lines of descent. In 2010 Stace adopted, for the third edition of his *New Flora*, the molecular classification of flowering plants that was published the previous year by the international Angiosperm Phylogeny Group (APG III). In consequence, I have rearranged my list of plants that were known to Clare in order to bring it into line with Stace's third edition, though not without regret over the trouble these changes are bound to cause readers. Now that so many books meant to guide our first steps in the identification of wild flowers have gone over to simpler categories of classification such as habitat or season, non-specialist readers already have their work cut out to track down a plant in the family-by-family arrangement of a traditional flora, and may well feel distinctly cross at having to cope with further change – for example, with the near disappearance from *A John Clare Flora* of the once familiar Lily family, now that its one-time Bluebells, onions and the like have been dispersed through several other families (see pp. 163 and 174–7). The only palliation I can offer is, firstly, that such recent changes, based as they are on totally objective data as opposed to observed features, are in all probability permanent, and secondly, that I have tried to ensure quick and easy access to individual items by making the index to the plants named as comprehensive and as user-friendly as possible.

Clare's experience of his countryside's flowers and his evocations of that experience in his own words as they appear on every page of this flora are its prime concerns; and, like the linear ordering of the work, the form of these quotations calls for some explanation and, it may be, justification. For the most part Clare wrote as he spoke, which is one reason why his writings are so alive today. Early transcribers or publishers of his poetry often sought to 'correct' his spelling, punctuation and grammar, and occasionally his metre, whereas the editors of the Oxford English Texts edition print those of his poems that have survived in manuscript exactly as he wrote them. Modern editors of selections from his verse for the most part choose a middle course; they regularise spellings and often punctuation as well, but do not interfere with grammar or metre.

There have been some fierce arguments over this matter of regularisation. My own position is that everything depends on the context in which the quotations are presented. If it is literary-critical, a modest degree of regularisation, while making no difference to the way the poetry sounds, keeps at bay the false image of Clare as a semi-literate yokel and serves to put him, in readers' eyes, on an equal footing with poets who were his contemporaries. If however the context is mainly a biographical one, as it is here, quotations need to be in a form that brings readers as close as possible to the poet himself at the moment of composition, and for this reason I have faithfully followed the Oxford English Texts edition – with two small exceptions. One is that I have everywhere written out the ampersand ('&') as 'and' – which is what we hear in our heads. The other is that, bearing in mind that readers may well want to hunt down the source of a quotation in an edition other than the Oxford one, I have used standard spelling for the titles of poems: 'A Rhapsody', for instance, is easier to look up than 'A Raphsody'. In addition I have occasionally added a gloss for an ambiguous spelling, such as 'were' for 'where'.

By keeping interventions between Clare's words and the reader to this minimum, I have sought to preserve the immediacy which is for me the most characteristic thing about his writings. He is unique among poets in that he conceives of the life forms that surround him as themselves the images of poetry, so that the experience of seeing them (and often too of hearing, smelling, touching and tasting them), together with the feelings that they arouse, forms a continuum with their transposition into words which as often as not were assembled and even written down on the spot. It is a way of working that makes him the most transparent of poets: a finder, not a maker. It means that for him there is no fallow period followed by a recollection in tranquillity that will enable him to shape his reflections into an artefact. This in itself might seem to set him apart from other Romantic poets such as Keats, Tennyson and Yeats. Yet when I search my memory for one of Clare's living moments of interaction between man and plant that may serve as an ending to this Introduction, there comes back most persistently his record of one encounter that sets him firmly in the Romanticism of the age while, at the same time, it demonstrates the uniqueness of his response to the growing life all round him.

Clare once found a poppy that was as blue as a cornflower. 'It was a miracle', he wrote years later, recalling an amazement similar to that experienced by Gerard Novalis when the Blue Flower appeared to him in a dream and so provided European Romanticism with a symbol of unattainable beauty that was to remain potent through many literary generations. Clare however was wide awake. He was in fact hoeing between rows of vegetables at the time, which is likely to have been in the summer of 1811 during his gardening apprenticeship, or (less probably) in the summer of 1817 when – his parents being near to destitution and in danger of eviction from their cottage – he had returned to the grounds of Burghley House as an extra labourer. What is certain is that the poppy, a self-seeded escape from the pleasure garden, was real enough: it may have been the result of an early and unrecorded introduction of *Meconopsis aculeata* from Kashmir. And for all his sense of the miraculous, Clare responded not with *Sehnsucht* but with direct action: he took home a poppy-head and raised a first generation of plants from its seeds. Shortly after either of the two possible dates, he had to leave his own garden for a time in other hands and in consequence, as he records, 'lost' his blue poppy. But his response, in its directness and simplicity, exemplifies the same deep and instinctive confidence in the green world's powers of self-renewal that underlies all his 'nature' poetry and shows itself in his numberless evocations of the wild flowers he loved. It is an absolute faith that the woods and fields of his own countryside have

> nothing mortal in them – their decay
> Is the green life of change to pass away
> And come again in blooms revivified
>> ('All nature has a feeling…', LP, 219)

– a faith that is for us to uphold.

PROEM: LICHENS, ALGAE AND MOSSES

As well as the flowering plants implied by its name, a Flora traditionally includes two groups of plants that immediately preceded the flowerers in the course of evolution: ferns with their allies; and conifers. But Clare's experience of the green kingdom, like that of most people, also embraced the more 'primitive' plant groups such as algae, lichens and mosses, so this preliminary note touches on his knowledge of these.

One of these groups, the lichens (plate 16), is in fact half in and half out of the plant kingdom, since each of its members represents a mutually beneficial union between an alga and a fungus. Early nineteenth-century botanists, 'men of science and of taste' as Clare calls them, were fascinated by the seemingly endless variety of lichens on stone and wood revealed by the much improved lenses of the time: – 'The bare rock has its blossom's sweet / The micriscope espies' ('Spring' ['The sweet spring now is come'ng'], LP, 172) – and like him many of them would have kept from childhood painful memories of one particular lichen:

The hugh oaks splintered trunks appear	*huge*
When spring is in her early pride	
As they were whitewashed every year	
Upon their bleak and northern side	
So when I clomb the puddocks nest	*kite's*
I chose the side that faced the south	
As dust rubbed off agen the breast	
Stived hot and bitter in the mouth	*crowded in*
('Birds Nesting', MP II, 166).	

It is clear from this that at some time in his birdnesting boyhood Clare, half way up an oak tree, had found himself in a cloud of the bitter-tasting powder (made up of cells ready for the vegetative stage of reproduction) that is given off by the crusty white lichen *Pertusaria amara*.

Leafy tree lichens, such as we now think of as indicators of low air pollution, are called 'lungwort' by Clare in one of his early prose pieces

'The Woodman' (NH, 6) where he writes of them having jagged leaves and growing on oak and ash trunks. He appears to have used the name, which at that stage he could have got from an early botanical work such as Gerard's *Herbal* or John Parkinson's *Theatrum Botanicum*, for any leafy species. A jotting about birds' nesting materials that he made in the mid 1820s notes that long-tailed tits construct their nests from a 'grey lichen' (NH, 116); in the colloquial language he was using about this time for *The Shepherd's Calendar* this appears as the 'grey tree moss' with which 'Bum barrels' build their 'curious pudding-nest' ('May', MP I, 71). Grainger tentatively suggests *Parmelia physodes*.

Clare would have been young when he encountered a true alga by fishing some of the green hot-weather film known as 'blanket weed' out of a Helpston pond and discovering it to be what he would describe as 'a sort of hairy moss' ('Rhymes in the Meadows', MP III, 577). In fact it is a member of the algal genus *Cladophora*.

Mosses themselves were the focus of keen study in the early part of the nineteenth century. Aware that botanists were distinguishing hundreds of species, 'in whose meaness genius sees / A world of wonders shine', Clare gave them a voice of their own in the 'Song of Praise' he based on the 148th Psalm (EP II, 605). Yet he never troubled with these distinctions himself. Like any other outdoor worker, he thought of moss in general terms as something comfortable to sit on. In 'The Flitting', one of his finest poems, its persistence stands for poetry's durability, as represented by the Psalms of the young shepherd David, in contrast to the vanished pomp of David, King of Israel:

> But passions of sublimity
> Belong to plain and simpler things
> And David underneath a tree
> Sought when a shepherd Salems springs
>
> Where moss did into cushions spring
> Forming a seat of velvet hue
> A small unnoticed trifling thing
> To all but heavens hailing dew

And Davids crown hath passed away
Yet poesy breaths his shepherd skill
His palace lost – and to this day
The little moss is blooming still   (MP III, 482–3).

FERNS AND THEIR ALLIES

Swept up by his Milton Hall friend Henderson into an early phase of the nineteenth century's Great Fern Craze, Clare in the winter of 1824–25 was 'passionat[e]ly bent' (*Letters*, 313) on making his own collection, and the journal he kept at the time contains many references to finding and identifying ferns and transplanting them into his garden. But the Helpston area, which has one of the lowest rainfalls in Britain, was not fern country. Moreover, the land drainage consequent upon the Enclosures was beginning to tell on fern populations, as the poet implies when he visits 'an old favourite spot in Oxey wood that used to be smotherd with Ferns' (NH, 230). Discouraged, perhaps, by his collection being 'nearly scorchd up' in a heat-wave in the following July (NH, 250), Clare appears to have grown quickly out of his pteridomania. All the same, memories of that winter's fern hunting fed into his later poetry and especially into the double sonnet, 'The Clump of Fern', the second part of which records a joy of discovery identical to that he felt at other seasons when he came upon a nest or a special flower:

Here underneath the stiles moss covered post
A little bunch of fern doth thrive and spring
Hid from the noisey wind and coming frost
Like late reared young neath the wood piegons wing
Ive seen beneath the furze bush clumps of ling
So beautiful in pinky knotts of bloom
That made the inmost hearts emotions breath
A favourite love for the unsocial heath
That gives man no inviting hopes to come
To fix his dwelling and disturb the scene
So in my lonliness of mood this green
Large clump of crimpled fern leaves doth bequeath
Like feelings – and whenever wanderers roam
Some little scraps of happiness is seen   (MP IV, 307).

Adder's-tongue family, OPHIOGLOSSACEAE

ADDER'S-TONGUE, *Ophioglossum vulgatum* (plate 6)

Among the plants gathered by Clare's 'Village Doctress' in the poem with that title was 'Famed ea[r]thern tongue that sprouts on april baulks' (MP III, 337). Quite unlike true ferns in appearance, the plant gets its name ('earthern' means 'heath-dweller', i.e. adder) from its spore-bearing spike or 'tongue' within a bright green sheath that resembles a snake's mouth; spike and sheath are actually the two blades of a single leaf. The plant was famed for its healing properties, and from it the Doctress, instructed by Gerard's *Herbal*, would have made the ointment known as the green oil of charity. Now far from common, it can still be found in an area of former ridge-and-furrow once crisscrossed by the green strips called 'baulks' and today protected as the SSSI and nature reserve called Southorpe Meadow, which is near Helpston.

Horsetail family, EQUISETACEAE

MARSH HORSETAIL, *Equisetum palustre*

Descendants of the coal forest giants that were the first plants to stand up on their own, horsetails are allied to ferns in reproducing by spores, not seeds. Since Clare's horsetails have 'bushey tufts' ('Wanderings in June', MP I, 313), are bristly enough for children to call them 'bottle b[r]ushes' ('May', MP I, 70) and are always spoken of by him as growing near water, they are most probably the Marsh Horsetail, *E. palustre*.

Bracken family, DENNSTAEDTIACEAE

BRACKEN, *Pteridium aquilinum*

Clare usually calls this 'brake', though 'bracken' becomes more common in his later verse: 'Dear to thee was mild showers / And heaths o' green bracan' he wrote on the back of his own portrait (LP, 697).

He took equal delight in the brilliant green of the young fronds that uncurled at the time when Bluebells and Early-purple Orchids could be found 'neath the featherd brake' ('The Wild-flower Nosegay', EP II, 411) and in the golden haze that dead Bracken added to a wintry landscape –

I love to see the old heaths withered brake
Mingle its crimpled leaves with furze and ling
('Emmonsales Heath in Winter', MP IV, 286).

Spleenwort family, ASPLENIACEAE

SPLEENWORTS, *Asplenium* spp.

In November 1824 Clare, having looked in vain for the Hart's-tongue fern, *A. scolopendrium*, noted in his journal that the most likely place to find it was inside a well shaft although he had also come across it 'about the badger holes in open Copy wood' (NH, 206). So he must have been pleased when, a week later, Henderson sent him a specimen he had found growing on the brickwork of a well shaft (NH, 204, 207; see also 62). Both sites were characteristically dim-lit, for this is a shade-loving fern. Early in the last century Druce believed it to be on the decline in Clare country. But because it has benefited from our failure to keep up coppicing, we can still sometimes share the pleasure Clare felt at the sight of its gleaming, undivided leaves 'shining rich and resolutely green' on a woodland floor ('The Spindle Tree', MP IV, 330).

Other ferns of this genus, because they looked a little like the prized Maidenhair that at the time grew only in the west of Britain, were miscalled 'maidenhairs' in eighteenth century guides such as John Hill's *Family Herbal*, which Clare owned. In December 1824 he found 'the White Maiden Hair of Hill' (NH, 209) in Oxey Wood. John Hill's fern is Wall-rue, *A. ruta-muraria*, which is still common in the district. Likewise, the 'black maiden hair' (NH, 226) that Clare hunted for in March 1825 was probably Black Spleenwort, *A. adiantum-nigrum*. More problematic is his description of a fern with 'a leaf very like the hemlock but of a much paler green' (NH, 62), but this was perhaps the true Lady-fern, *Athyrium filix-femina*, of the family Woodsiaceae, which is not uncommon near Clare's home in the Soke.

Marsh Fern family, THELIPTERIDACEAE

MARSH FERN, *Thelypteris palustris*

Clare was highly pleased in November 1824 to learn that Henderson had discovered a new species of fern 'growing among the bogs on Whittlesea Mere', and with good reason; a week later there arrived 'a parcel of Ferns and flowers from Henderson' that included 'the Lady fern growing at whittlesea Meer' (NH, 204, 207). The Mere was a large expanse of water lying some dozen miles south-east of Milton Hall in what was then Huntingdonshire. It was drained in 1850. The name 'Lady fern', a translation of '*Filix foemina*', was originally applied to Bracken, *Pteridium aquilinum*, and was still not the standard name of *Athyrium filix-femina* (see previous entry) in Clare's day. The most probable identification for the fern from Whittlesey Mere, which accords well with the phrase 'among the bogs', is Marsh Fern, *Thelypteris palustris*. This was evidently favoured by Terry Wells, who attributed records of it there to Clare in 1825 as well as to Newbould in 1846; it was lost with the draining of the Mere. *Thelypteris* is the Greek equivalent of '*Filix foemina*'.

Buckler-fern family, DRYOPTERIDACEAE

BUCKLER-FERNS, *Dryopteris* spp.

Clare describes Male-fern, *D. filix-mas*, which he knew by the name of 'fox fern', as 'the commonest of all about here' (NH, 217), and it remains plentiful in his neighbourhood. Some early and fragmentary lines 'To the Fox Fern' attempt to capture its woodland setting:

near w[h]ere summers light
Buried in boughs forgets its glare and round thy crimped leaves
Feints in a quiet dimness... (EP I, 469).

In December 1824 Clare took a similar fern which he had found 'in Harrisons close dyke by the wood lane' (NH, 210) to Milton Hall, where Henderson must have produced, either off his own bat or with recourse to a book, the name 'thorn pointed fern'. This could refer to the dense covering of pointed scales on the leaf-stalks of Broad Buckler-fern, *D. dilatata*, or less probably to the three-times or even four-times divided fronds that characterise this fairly common species that can often be found in ditches.

Polypody family, POLYPODIACEAE

COMMON POLYPODY, *Polypodium vulgare*

Clare found polypody ferns growing on old willow trees – a favourite habitat – in Helpston's Lolham Lane (NH, 209). He believed that there were two species in the district, but the probability is that the small and large specimens he found were all Common Polypody. This fern has become less common than it was because the stone walls that are its other favourite habitat are now kept discouragingly well repaired.

CONIFERS

Coniferous trees are not native to the Soke of Peterborough, so the ones known to Clare would almost certainly have been planted. This meant that for the most part they were only to be found on big estates. Clare knew two of these well. His working life as a gardener began around 1810 at Burghley House, just south of Stamford, and in 1822 he became friendly with the upper servants of Milton Hall near Peterborough and a frequent visitor to its demesne. The parks and gardens of both great houses had been landscaped in the previous century: Burghley by 'Capability' Brown, and Milton by Humphrey Repton, who had a special liking for the spikiness of conifers. So, it seems, had the owner of the much smaller estate of Holywell House over the Lincolnshire border, whose garden with its many evergreens Clare explored on a visit that he recorded both in verse and – very amusingly – in prose ('Hollywell', EP II, 42; *By Himself*, 129).

Pine family, PINACEAE

SPRUCES, *Picea* spp.

A walk in the fields, Clare insists in the poem with that title, far outshines a walk taken 'Thro flowers newly planted and spruce evergreens' (MP III, 379). 'Spruce' here sounds like a half-pun, suggestive of the various species of *Picea* introduced from Europe and America from the fourteenth century onwards. Clare is inclined to call them all 'firs', a term he uses also for the Scots Pine and for true firs, *Abies*. So we cannot identify with any certainty the 'firs' that are the subject of the one short poem he devotes to them, though their tapering form and blue-green colour suggest the Norway Spruce, *P. abies* (our modern Christmas tree), which by Clare's time was a well established plantation tree:

> The firs that taper into twigs and wear
> The rich blue green of summer all the year
> Softening the roughest tempests almost calm

And offering shelter ever still and warm
To the small path that travels underneath
Where loudest winds almost as summers breath
Scarce fans the weed that lingers green below
When others out of doors are lost in frost and snow
And sweet the music trembles on the ear
As the wind suthers through each tiney spear
Make shifts for leaves and yet so rich they show
Winter is almost summer where they grow   (MP V, 16).

The stress here on shelter and protection is significant, since the poem was written after Clare's 'flitting' to Northborough, where he felt himself exposed to a bleak fenland landscape. Perhaps he was remembering the lavish planting of the Milton Hall grounds and the protective friendships he enjoyed there.

EUROPEAN LARCH, *Larix decidua* (plate 4)

Though larches had been introduced into England two hundred years previously, Clare seems not to have encountered them before he was moved to the Northampton asylum. When he did so he revelled in their colourfulness. 'There's no flowers more red, than the flowers of the larch' he writes of the minute female cones which would grow into 'Cones o' purple rich studding the starry leaves green' ('Spring Violets' ['Push that rough maple…'], LP, 308; 'Sweet Spring', LP, 619). Unlike most conifers, larches are deciduous; in one of his last poems, 'The Winter's Come', Clare celebrates the tree's golden autumn foliage, 'like the colour of the sun / That paled sky in the Autumn seem'd to burn' (LP, 928).

CEDAR-OF-LEBANON, *Cedrus libani*

This gets only a passing mention from Clare, in his paraphrase of a biblical passage in which it occurs ('Balaam's Parable', LP, 107). But he would have known this magnificent tree, which had been introduced to Britain around 1630, since by the end of the eighteenth century scarcely any large

English estate was without a specimen or two.

SCOTS PINE, *Pinus sylvestris*

'The mountain fir that waves in pride / Oerleukin half the land' ('Scotland',
LP, 424) figures in a number of Clare's song-lyrics that attempt a Scottish
setting and a Scots diction, along with lassies 'Straight as the firdale in
the wood' ('The girl I love...', LP, 668). 'Dale' means deal or timber, a
reminder that for centuries Scotland's indigenous pine forests were ravaged
to supply England with masts and planks for shipbuilding.

Self-sown Scots pines are frequent on English heaths today, but in
Clare's time the forebears of these would often have been landmark trees,
planted to guide Highland cattle drovers like those he vividly describes in
The Shepherd's Calendar:

> men so oddly clad
> In petticoats of banded plad
> Wi blankets oer their shoulders slung
> To camp at night the fields among
> When they rest on commons stop
> And blue cap like a stocking top
> Cockt oer their faces summer brown
> Wi scarlet tazzeles on the crown　　　('July', MP I, 91).

If the drovers' southward road was the old Roman one called King Street it
would have led them to the common of Ailsworth ('Emmonsails') Heath,
where they could pasture and water their herd.

Yew family, TAXACEAE

YEW, *Taxus baccata*

Clare would have known this only as a tree planted in churchyards, a locale
he exploits in such 'Gothick' passages as the account in 'Solitude' of his
visit to a ruined abbey, with its 'shades of gloomy yew / Dolfull hung

wi mourning green' (EP II, 346). The foliage is less doleful when used for Christmas decorations ('December', MP I, 157). But regrettably Clare has no lines about this wonderful tree that can compare with the 'fruitful cloud and living smoke' of pollen that breaks from Tennyson's yew 'When flower is feeling after flower'.

FLOWERING PLANTS – DICOTS

Water-lily family, NYMPHAEACEAE

Long recognised to have been in existence prior to all other flowering plants in Britain, where their pollen has been found in Jurassic rocks, Water-lilies are one of a small number of plant families that preceded the divergence of dicotyledons and monocotyledons, and are classed as 'Pre-dicots' in the molecular system of classification. All subsequent dicot families are 'Eu-dicots', i.e. true dicots.

WHITE WATER-LILY, *Nymphaea alba*
YELLOW WATER-LILY, *Nuphar lutea*

In Clare's day both the White and the Yellow Water-lily thrived in the slow-flowing River Welland as well as in the many ponds and small lakes round Helpston, where they were 'In dangerous deeps yet out of dangers way' ('Water-Lilies', MP IV, 587) and so safe from children's attempts to reach them even with 'the longest pole' ('The Water Lilies', LP, 26). The leaves of the White Water-lily, 'green isles of beauty' ('Shadows of Taste', MP III, 304), fascinated him both by the copper gleam of their first appearance and by the oiliness that attracted hosts of insects –

> The leaves like boats float upward and are dry
> If dropples plash upon them from the spring
> Of leaping fish they scarce a moment lie
> But roll like water from the morehens wing
> Its oily green still sunny as before
> ('The Meadow Lake', MP IV, 579–80).

Clare once managed to get hold of a root of the Yellow Water-lily (which in a late poem, 'The Walk', LP, 306, he calls 'the large marsh marygold') and like many another gardener planted it in an old water butt (NH, 197).

Poppy family, PAPAVERACEAE

COMMON POPPY, *Papaver rhoeas* (plates 14 and 15)

Clare grew up calling these colourful and most prolific of cornfield weeds 'headaches' (from the supposed effect of smelling them), although in his first published volume he avoids this homely name by terming them 'crimson corn-flowers' ('Elegy', EP I, 121). He reverts to 'headaches' in several nostalgic late lyrics, but in between, in *The Midsummer Cushion*, they are always 'poppies'. Massed together, they are a blazing fire; mixed with brassy Charlock, an army on the march; surrounded by Cornflowers and Corncockles, a sunset sky. Only once does he touch upon the seeds that are the source of all this brilliance, and that in a late poem: as autumn approaches

> The roses to hips are gone The poppy seeds every one
> Come wi' straw bonnet on
> > ('Come Nanny dear near me', LP, 750)

– the bonnet being the top of the seed capsule, very like the flat, 'bergère', straw hats of eighteenth-century portraits, later known as Dolly Vardens.

WELSH and THORNY POPPIES, *Meconopsis* spp.

In his 1823 notes on *Flora Domestica* and in the afterword to them that Grainger calls Natural History Letter Ia (NH, 21, 25), as well as in a passage of about the same time intended for the continuation of his autobiographical sketches (*By Himself*, 74), Clare recalls that when he was working in the vegetable garden of Burghley House he came across a yellow poppy and a cornflower-blue poppy 'growing wild among the vegetables'. The yellow one would have been the Welsh Poppy, *M. cambrica*, and since the species is not native to the East Midlands the one that Clare found must have escaped from the flower garden. But the appearance of a blue poppy in Britain in or before 1817–18, when Clare last worked at Burghley, raises a fascinating possibility.

All *Meconopsis* species other than Welsh Poppies come from the Himalayas, the most famous blue one being *M. betonicifolia* from the eastern ranges, which was 'discovered' in late Victorian times and successfully established in British gardens in the 1920s. But it was not the first blue poppy known to westerners. Grainger suggests – tentatively but I believe correctly – that the plant Clare found was the Thorny Poppy, *M. aculeata*, from Kashmir. It has been thought hitherto that this species was first described for a British public in 1834 by J. F. Royle of the East India Company, after which attempts – presumably unsuccessful – were made to introduce it in the 1850s and 1860s. However its medicinal reputation in India was such that it is highly probable that its seeds were brought into Europe at an earlier date; and when it proved to be beautiful into the bargain, Burghley's owner, the Marquess of Exeter, may well have wanted it for his flower garden. Had his head gardener succeeded in establishing it, there would have been a buzz among nurserymen and owners of large gardens, so we must assume he failed – as too did Clare, who took home seeds that germinated, but 'lost' the plant in its second year.

GREATER CELANDINE, *Chelidonium majus* (plate 15)

Despite its being depicted on the Wordsworth memorial at Grasmere, this attractive wild flower, with distinctively divided leaves and four yellow petals as frail as a poppy's, is no relation to the Lesser Celandine. Helpston locals knew it as 'wart weed', being convinced, as was Clare himself, that the yellow juice or latex from its stems effectively removed warts (NH, 16–17).

COMMON FUMITORY, *Fumaria officinalis*

For all the charm of its trailing pink-and-purple flowers, Common Fumitory was an agricultural nuisance in Clare's time. He describes it as 'a little pretty plant among our corn fields … which I have known the young girls get in weeding time to make a wash of to beautify the skin' (NH, 18) and in the May section of *The Shepherd's Calendar* (MP I, 64) he shows them doing just that, because 'Superstition with all her deformity is a very poetical personage with me and I love to dwell on such trifles' (NH, 19).

The family to which the fumitories once belonged, Fumariaceae, is now included in Papaveraceae.

Barberry family, BERBERIDACEAE

BARREN-WORT, *Epimedium alpinum*

'[H]ealth is the root of happiness and like the plant called "Barrenwort" it seldom produces a blossom', Clare remarks in a letter to his publisher (*Letters*, 347). He was recalling John Hill's explanation of the name in his *Family Herbal* – that this plant's small but beautiful flowers appear only in deep shade. Certainly its preferred method of reproducing itself is by creeping rhizomes, and this has made modern garden varieties of *Epimedium* a favourite form of ground cover. But the English name in fact relates to its supposed power as a contraceptive.

BARBERRY, *Berberis vulgaris*

Early in 1825 Clare cut off a sucker of Barberry in woodland and planted it in his garden (NH, 220), where he might hope to enjoy the colour and perhaps the taste – if well sweetened – of its berries. This suggests the plant was a native of the district before its prickliness made it popular for Enclosure hedging. But already it was coming under suspicion as a possible source of the dreaded wheat-rust: in a note on 'the mildew', written probably in September 1824, Clare records that some 'Farmer-philosophers … are of opinion that a barberry bush standing in a field is the cause' (NH, 102). Later in the nineteenth century, when the plant was found to be a secondary host to the fungus causing the disease, Barberry hedges were everywhere grubbed out. Surprisingly, a twenty-metre stretch of one has survived on the edge of Helpston village and is now protected.

Buttercup family, RANUNCULACEAE

Told that buttercups were closely related to larkspurs, John Ruskin declared 'I can't believe it; and won't'. The family Ranunculaceae has certainly developed some varied forms in its long evolutionary history. Clare alludes to twelve genera that occur wild or occasionally naturalised in Britain, and among them are some of his favourite flowers.

MARSH-MARIGOLD, *Caltha palustris* (plate 9)

Clare sometimes calls this brilliant and showy flower by the formal, if misleading, name of 'marsh-marigold', but he never uses the now widespread 'kingcup', since for him this means either a buttercup or a Lesser Celandine. His preferred names are the Northamptonshire 'horse blob' and 'mare blob'; a line in 'Last of March' – 'The horse blob swells its golden ball' (EP II, 472) – suggests that he thought of 'blob' as descriptive of the flower in bud. Clare's poetic *persona*, the village minstrel Lubin, is quick to notice the plant's disappearance from previously marshy places drained as a result of the Enclosures, when he

> Marks the stopt brook and mourns oppresions power
> And thinks how once he waded in each slough
> To crop the yellow 'horse blobs' early flower
> ('The Village Minstrel', EP II, 168).

Matters are worse today in Clare country, where, according to Terry Wells, the Marsh-marigold is 'uncommon and decreasing'.

There is a cultivated double variety of *C. palustris*. At Milton Hall, Henderson had a single plant of it which, in a St Martin-like gesture, he lifted and divided with Clare.

HELLEBORES, *Helleborus* spp.

Despite their rarity in the area today, Clare could have found both British hellebores locally: Culpeper tells us that the Green Hellebore, *H. viridis*, favoured Northamptonshire; and the Stinking Hellebore, *H. foetidus*, though mainly a wild plant of southern England, had long been grown in gardens elsewhere. Keats, for one, looked at growing hellebores, for he refers to the backward droop of the divided lower leaves – the feature that gives the plant its English name of 'bear's foot'. Clare's sole mention of it, in 'The Inconstant Shepherd', where jealous thoughts are said to be 'worse than hellebore and poison berries are' (MP IV, 87), sounds bookish in comparison: behind it stretches a long line of allusions in Latin and English poetry to hellebore's deadly powers.

WINTER ACONITE, *Eranthis hyemalis* (plate 16)

Though it is widely naturalised today, Clare probably knew this as a cultivated flower that was the first to brighten his garden in the dark days of winter. In 'Flowers: a Poem' (MP II, 198), it peeps before the end of January, and in *The Shepherd's Calendar* there is enough of it by March to keep hive bees busy

> venturing short flight w[h]ere the snow drop hings
> Its silver bell – and winter aconite
> Wi buttercup like flowers that shut at night
> And green leaf frilling round their cups of gold
> Like tender maiden muffld from the cold   (MP I, 49).

MONK'S-HOODS, *Aconitum* spp.

Monk's-hood, *A. napellus*, blooms 'darkly blue' in the June garden of *The Shepherd's Calendar* (MP I, 81), but Wolf's-bane, *A. lycoctonum*, which is yellow, occurs only in a prose note about 'very poisonous flowers such as hen bane wolfs bane Monkhood &c &c' (NH, 271). Grainger thought that Clare would not have distinguished two *Aconitum* species, and that by 'wolfs bane' he here means the Winter Aconite. But John Abercrombie's *The Gardener's Companion*, which he owned, lists both species; and there is no hint in Clare's several tender allusions to Winter Aconites that he thought of them as poisonous.

LARKSPUR, *Consolida ajacis*

In *The Shepherd's Calendar*, 'tall tuft larkheels featherd thick wi flowers' are among the cottage garden favourites the village girls pick for their clipping posies at sheep-shearing time ('June', MP I, 81).

ANEMONES, *Anemone* spp.

The Helpston children's name for Wood Anemones, *A. nemorosa*, was 'lady smocks' (see p. 96), and Clare once alludes to them as 'smell smocks', in reference to their musky smell, though by the time he wrote 'Cowper Green' (EP II, 183) he knew them as 'anemones'. Of their many appearances in his poetry, the most memorable is perhaps that in 'The Wood lark's Nest':

Ive often wondered when agen my feet
She fluttered up and fanned the anemonie
That blossomed round in crowds – how birds could be
So wise to find such hidden homes again   (MP IV, 322).

The plant's 'pretty, drooping weeping flowers' and 'clipt frilled leaves' figure in the late poem 'Wood Anemone' (LP, 497), where Clare speaks of the flowers as white, purple and yellow. Most Wood Anemones are as white as if they had been 'Dyd in winters snow and ryhme' ('Cowper Green', EP II, 183) while others are flushed or streaked with purple, but the Yellow Anemone, *A. ranunculoides*, is a Mediterranean plant, as Joseph Henderson had told Clare many years previously. Henderson's employer Lord Milton brought it back from his Grand Tour (NH, 24), so here we may have a memory, in Clare's asylum days, of the native and the introduced species growing together in the grounds of Milton Hall.

In June 1825 Clare admired a 'Scarlet Anemonie' (NH, 245) in the garden of his one-time employer Mrs Bellairs, who sent him seed from it two months later. This suggests that her plant was Crown Anemone, *A. coronaria*, which is easily propagated in this way. See the entry under 'Garden Peony' (p. 41).

LIVERLEAF, *Hepatica nobilis*

The cultivated spring flower *Hepatica nobilis* is most commonly blue, so a white specimen was a welcome gift in the days when Clare had his own garden (NH, 23), and he was struck by the sight of a double pink one in the asylum garden at Northampton ('The healthfull mind...', LP, 232). He knew the plant as 'hepatica', which in one of his last poems he spells 'patty kay' – a touching, if unconscious, recall of the wife he was never to see again ('The spring is come...', LP, 1104).

PASQUEFLOWER, *Pulsatilla vulgaris* (plate 5)

On 25 March 1825, Clare wrote of the 'Anemonie pulsitilis of botanists', which he had just found in flower:

> I coud almost fancy that this blue anenonie sprang from the blood or dust of the romans for ... it grows on the roman bank agen swordy well and did grow in great plenty but the plough that destroyer of wild flowers has rooted it out of its long inherited dwelling it grows also on the roman bank agen Burghley Park in Barnack Lordship it is a very fine flower and is easily cultivated by transporting some of its own soil with it... (NH, 61).

Clare was lucky to live in a calcareous area where the Pasqueflower grew, as it still grows. But the destroyer of wild flowers has continued its work, and today this glorious flower is restricted locally to a single site, Barnack Hills and Holes. Sadly, Clare makes no mention of it anywhere in his poetry.

TRAVELLER'S-JOYS, *Clematis* spp.

Early in their friendship, Henderson returned to Clare the number of the *London Magazine* containing 'Wanderings in June'. He praised the poem, but objected to Clare's allusion to a 'goat's beard wreath' (MP I, 314): 'old man's beard' was what was meant, 'goat's beard' being the name of a totally different plant. In fact Clare already knew Traveller's-joy,

C. vitalba (plate 7), as 'old man's beard', though he slips back into 'Goat's beard' in one very late poem ('What beauties the summer discloses...', LP, 1064). Henderson, however, never managed to dissuade his friend from calling the distinctive, whiskery fruits 'flowers'. Still, one thing he did succeed in impressing upon Clare was that Honeysuckle twines to the right and Old-man's-beard to the left (NH, 210).

Though the native Traveller's-joy is sometimes called 'Virgin's bower', Clare seems to use the name 'virginbower' for the pure white and scented *C. flammula* from southern Europe; in a very early poem, 'The Wish', he pictures 'virginbower' round an arbour in his ideal garden (EP I, 46).

BUTTERCUPS, *Ranunculus* spp.

Druce, in his list of Clare's plants, implies that the poet distinguished Bulbous Buttercup, *R. bulbosus*, from Meadow Buttercup, *R. acris*, and that he called the first 'kingcup' and the second 'buttercup' or 'crowfoot' or 'yellow cup'. But the only distinction Clare himself makes – for instance in his allusion to 'the taller buttercup' (NH, 41) which 'proudly leaves the grass to meet the sun' ('Pleasures of Spring', MP III, 57) – is that between such summer-flowering species and the spring-flowering Lesser Celandine, now placed in a distinct genus; see the next entry.

'Buttercup' only came into use for summer species of *Ranunculus* in the middle of the eighteenth century, and Clare tends to stick to 'crowflower', 'crowfoot' or 'kingcup' ('the bell of the crowfoot the king cup of flowers' – ''Tis Midsummer Eve', MP II, 205). Two early poems use the flower to point the moral that showiness without the virtue represented by fragrance leads to rejection ('On a wither'd Crowflower', EP I, 96; 'The Contrast', EP I, 347), but in later poems

> slender king cups burnished with the dew
> Of mornings early hours
> Like gold yminted new   ('Summer Images', MP III, 152),

are chiefly seen as lovers' offerings.

Two other species of *Ranunculus* appear in Clare's poems, though he has no names for them. One is the Corn Buttercup, *R. arvensis*, a weed of agriculture with distinctive, clinging fruits, which was still 'widely distributed' in 1936 but has now disappeared from Helpston and indeed from almost everywhere else:

Stave acres little yellow weeds
The wheat fields constant blooms
That ripen into prickly seeds
For fairys curry combs   ('Fairy Things', MP II, 116).

The other is a water-crowfoot, perhaps the River Water-crowfoot, *R. fluitans*, which fits the description, in 'Poesy a-Maying', of dancing water flowers 'which lie / Where many a silver curdle boils and dribbles' (MP IV, 201).

LESSER CELANDINE, *Ficaria verna* (plates 2 and 3)

In a note on Elizabeth Kent's mention of the Lesser Celandine in her *Flora Domestica*, Clare writes: 'this is my "crow flower" and "buttercup" the childen often call them "golden daiseys" some of the common people know them like wise by the name of "pile wort" but none by the name of "little celadine"' (NH, 16). 'Pilewort' is sometimes used in Clare's later poetry; perhaps it was the agreed name among his fellow-inmates of the asylum.

Clare knew Wordsworth's poems about the Lesser Celandine, but whereas the elder poet uses the loss of its ability to close as a moving simile for old age, he himself tends to associate it, no less movingly, with children. In 'Spring' ('How beautiful the spring...') it 'shuts at eve like childern tired of play' (MP III, 30), and in his rewriting of this poem as 'Pleasures of Spring' he recalls the game in which children hold the shimmering flower under each other's chins to discover which of them will become rich:

It early comes and glads the shepherds eye

Like a bright star spring-tempted from the sky
Reflecting on its leaves the suns bright rays
That sets its pointed glories in a blaze
So bright that childerns fancies it decieves
Who think that sunshine settles in its leaves
And playful hold it neath each others chins
To see it stain with gold their lily skin
And he who seems to win the brightest spot
Feels future wealth and fortune as his lot
Ah happy childhood with that sunny brow
No wealth can match what nature gives thee now
And like these blossoms of the golden bloom
Thy spring *must* fade tho summers wealth *may* come   (MP III, 58).

COLUMBINE, *Aquilegia vulgaris*

'[H]oney-comb-like blossoms' of 'stone blue or deep night brown' figure among garden flowers in *The Shepherd's Calendar*, but Clare calls them 'adopted' because 'heaths still claim them w[h]ere they yet grow wild' ('June', MP I, 81–2), and elsewhere he writes that 'the stone blue and ruby red both grow among bushes in uncultivated spots' (NH, 18). All this colour has vanished from some terse, almost grim, verses composed after Clare's 'flitting', which relate a foray across the hostile-seeming landscape of the Fens, at the end of which 'We found the columbine so black / And dug and took a bundle back' ('We went a journey...', MP V, 386).

COMMON MEADOW-RUE, *Thalictrum flavum*

Druce calls this plant 'local' in Northamptonshire, naming Helpston as one place where it grew in his day. Writing in the mid-1830s (NH, 18), Clare says there is a meadow plant with columbine-like leaves that the children call 'tassle flower' because 'its flowers are clusters of thready tufts' (i.e. stamens – the petals are insignificant). He must have learnt the more usual name of this damp-loving species later on, because in one of his last poems

The hemlocks and keksies and Rue
Grow rank by the side of the flood
('What beauties the summer discloses…', LP, 1064).

Plane family, PLATANACEAE

LONDON PLANE, *Platanus × hispanica*

'[T]he hoary plane' Clare calls it in 'Spring' ('How beautiful the spring…', MP III, 39). 'Hoary' is unlikely to refer to the tree's longevity because that was hardly tested at the time: the first specimens to be introduced into England, planted at Ely in Cambridgeshire and still flourishing today, were then a mere century and a half old. The word more probably relates to the whitish patches left on the tree's trunk by the annual shedding of its bark – a feature that is said to help it withstand urban pollution and thus has made it the favourite species of those planting the capital's squares and avenues. But Clare did not have to wait for his visits to London before he encountered a plane tree. As an alternative manuscript reading, 'and rarer plane', suggests, *P. × hispanica* could be found as a cherished rarity in the Soke, most probably on one or both of the two great estates that he knew.

Box family, BUXACEAE

BOX, *Buxus sempervirens*

In England this is native only in southern counties, but it has long been popular with gardeners everywhere because it submits to any amount of clipping. The fragrance of 'box edged borders' which has comforted the old cottager in Clare's 'Pastoral Poesy' for sixty years (MP III, 584) must, however, have come from the flowers it protected, for Box itself has an acrid scent. In the autumn of 1824 Clare planted an edging of it round the native ferns he was beginning to collect (NH, 198): his nearest source of cuttings for this would have been the box trees in the Billings brothers' garden. His journal for the spring of 1825 follows the fortune of some dunnocks nesting in these trees, and he makes one of them the subject of his poem 'Hedge Sparrow':

> And in the snug clipt box tree green and round
> It makes a nest of moss and hair and lays
> When een the snow is lurking on the ground
> Its eggs in number five of greenish blue
> Bright beautiful and glossy shining shells…   (MP IV, 237).

Peony family, PAEONIACEAE

GARDEN PEONY, *Paeonia officinalis*

A white variety of this was the object of social finesse in June 1825, when Mrs Bellairs of Woodcroft Castle near Helpston, who had given Clare his first job as her ploughboy, came to see his garden and he in turn visited her garden, where he saw 'a Scarlet Anemonie and White Piony both very handsome'. Three days later he sent her a present of flowers, and by return was promised the two coveted varieties and Brompton Stocks into the bargain. He planted some anemone seeds in August: but we hear nothing more of the peony (NH, 244–6, 253).

Gooseberry family, GROSSULARIACEAE

GOOSEBERRY and CURRANTS, *Ribes* spp.

Three varieties of Gooseberry, *R. uva-crispa*, were among the fruit offered for sale on Sundays at the foot of Helpston's village cross,

> Green ruffs and raspberry reds and drops of gold
> That make mouths water often to behold
> > ('August', MP I, 127),

as were two varieties of Red Currant, *R. rubrum* – 'curran[t]s red and white on cabbage leaves' (MP I, 127). Black Currants, *R. nigrum*, Clare grew for himself: 'Home Happiness' gives us a glimpse of him walking round his garden on a summer evening, rubbing between his fingers a leaf of Black Currant, which 'when touched leaves a smell / That ladslove and sweet briar can hardly excell' (MP IV, 120).

Saxifrage family, SAXIFRAGACEAE

LONDONPRIDE, *Saxifraga × urbium*

The seventeenth-century revision of Gerard's *Herbal* uses the name 'London Pride' for the plant known today as Sweet-William. But two descriptive phrases in Clare's poetry, 'London tufts of many a mottld hue' in 'June' (MP I, 81) and 'Beds edged with … thrift and London pride' in 'Summer Ballad' (MP IV, 142), suggest that by his time a smaller and less showy plant bore the name, which it owed (according to R.C.A. Prior) to its having been brought into cultivation by 'Mr London of the firm of London and Wise, the celebrated royal gardeners'.

Stonecrop family, CRASSULACEAE

HOUSE-LEEK, *Sempervivum tectorum*

Was it on account of the rosettes of red-tipped leaves flaring beneath its pink flowers that for many centuries the House-leek was planted (it rarely seeds itself) on roofs all over Europe as a form of fire insurance? 'A Charm to quell the lightnings power', it adorns the roof of the typical cottagers Dobson and Judie in the poem named after them (EP I, 174).

STONECROPS, *Sedum* spp.

One of Clare's notes on the plants listed in Elizabeth Kent's *Flora Domestica* reads:

'*House Leek*' page 186 no cottage ridges about us is with out these as Superstition holds it out as a charm against lightning the lesser sort calld 'love in chains' is often seen in pots in cottage windows and a lesser sort still growing upon garden walls calld 'golden wire' is a favourite with the common people these 3 sorts are natives of every village with us (NH, 20).

It appears from this, and from a couple of allusions to 'yellow houseleek', that in his early poems Clare used the name 'houseleek' for three different plants – the 'real' House-leek of the previous entry, which has pink flowers; Reflexed Stonecrop, *Sedum rupestre*, which has yellow flowers that droop in the bud but then stand erect; and the smaller, fiercely yellow Biting Stonecrop, *S. acre*. Probably it is the last of these that provides the yellow flowers he rejoices to see on the roof beneath a column of blue smoke as he approaches his own cottage in 'Home' (EP II, 3) – at which point readers of Grigson's *The Englishman's Flora* may recall the name given in Dorset to both House-leek and Biting Stonecrop: 'welcome-home-husband-though-never-so-drunk'.

When, however, Clare got to Elizabeth Kent's entry for 'Sedum', he found that she called his love-in-chains and his golden wire 'stonecrop'. Accordingly in 'Childhood', written about 1830, he uses this name for the plant that 'on ruins comes / And hangs like golden balls', further identifying it in another version as 'Called love in chains by childern small' (MP III, 239). Elizabeth Kent's references to red-flowered garden sedums reminded Clare that their wild original, Orpine, *S. telephium*, was also to be found in woods round Helpston: but it was not, he adds, common (NH, 21–2). Today it is very rare.

Grape-vine family, VITACEAE

GRAPE-VINE, *Vitis vinifera*

'The Wish' (EP I, 47) is the teenage Clare's description of the home that he hoped one day to possess. This dream was never to be fulfilled; but he must at some time have planted, against a wall of either his Helpston or his Northborough cottage, a vine such as he had envisaged in that very early poem, since he recalled it on a grey evening in Northampton many years later – and poignantly, once more with hope:

> But the cottage that stood in a garden of flowers
> Where the vine and the woodbine climb'd up by the wall
> Twas there that I lived in my happiest hours
> Tis there I shall live when the strife is gone by…
>
> ("'Tis evening…', LP, 517).

Pea Family, FABACEAE

Most members of this family, which older readers will know as Leguminosae or even, because the flowers of all European species are winged like butterflies, as Papilionaceae, are the farmer's green allies. Some of them constitute richly nutritious fodder crops. In addition, beans have been known since Roman times to play a vital soil-enriching role in the rotation of crops, and in the late nineteenth century it was discovered that this is due to bacteria that they and other plants of this family harbour in their roots, and which are able to 'fix' nitrogen from the air. Like any human family it also has members whose opportunism undermines this good reputation.

BEANS, *Phaseolus* spp.

The French Bean, *P. vulgaris*, was a favourite crop in Clare's part of the world: there must have been a ready sale for horse fodder to the coaching inns on the Great North Road. 'Strewing wi swinging arms the pattering beans' ('March', MP I, 40), Clare in his labouring days would have lugged a heavy hopper along wet furrows in early spring, hoed repeatedly between the seedlings in the months that followed, and in August scythed and stooked plants which by then were discoloured and 'crackling' ('The Harvest Morning', EP I, 435). But when he strolled through bean-fields on Sundays in high summer he revelled in, and recorded in poem after poem, the plants' winged and 'Black eyed' blossoms, their 'luscious' scent, and their feathery feel as they sprawled over the path 'in rich disorder': a multisensory experience to which there might be added the music of church bells, so that movement, scent and chime all blended into one, and 'The waving blossoms seemed to throw / Their fragrance to the sound' ('Sabbath Bells' MP III, 574; see also 'The Beans in Blossom', MP IV, 191, and 'The Bean Field', LP, 574).

The scent from a nearby bean-field is enjoyed by the old couple whose dwelling is described in a poem that begins 'The little cottage stood alone', but the 'kidney bean' that they grow for themselves and that 'twines and towers / Up little poles in wreaths of scarlet flowers' is the Runner Bean, *P. coccineus* (MP V, 202).

SAINFOIN, *Onobrychis viciifolia*

Although this is a native species that can still be found today, Clare knew it in the more leafy, cultivated form in which it had been introduced as a fodder crop from the calcareous uplands of France: hence the French name, meaning 'healthy hay'. At his first use of the name he confused 'sainfoin' with 'cinquefoil', but the context – a prospect from rising ground of a many-coloured patchwork of crops, among them

> Square platts of clover red and white
> Scented wi summers warm delight
> And sinkfoil of a fresher stain
> ('A Sunday with Shepherds and Herdboys', MP II, 16)

– makes clear that he was looking at a field of bright pink *O. viciifolia*. He gets closer to the right name in a sonnet, written after his move to Northborough, which contrasts the Fen landscape where there is nothing to see but 'dykes and water flowers' with 'The glorious sight of sinkfoin grounds in flower' in the countryside he has just left ('The dreary fen…', MP V, 264).

KIDNEY VETCH, *Anthyllis vulneraria*
BIRD'S-FOOT-TREFOILS, *Lotus* spp.

Among the sights of late spring that Clare missed when he left Helpston in 1832 were 'little lambtoe bunches' in their 'red tinged and begolden dye'

('The Flitting', MP III, 485). 'Lambtoe', he had explained in his glossary to *The Village Minstrel*, meant 'kidney vetch, lady's finger' and the word certainly brings to mind the stubby seedpods, each surrounded by a woolly calyx, that bunch together in the dense heads of *Anthyllis vulneraria* – just as 'lady's finger' suggests an earlier stage in which each yellow flower can be seen as the tip of a delicate digit, emerging perhaps from white mittens. But twenty years on, the glossary of Northamptonshire words and phrases compiled in the 1840s by Anne Baker defined 'lamb toe' as 'probably another name for the Lotus corniculatus' – that is, the Common Bird's-foot-trefoil. And Clare, she adds, is her authority for this.

It could be that we are here looking at a change of meaning such as overtook 'bluebell' during Clare's lifetime (see p. 176). 'Names one may think more apt for *Anthyllis vulneraria* have been transferred to the Lotus', Grigson says in his discusssion of the seventy or so local terms for Bird's-foot-trefoil. However, the discrepancy between the two glossaries admits of another explanation, which is that 'lambtoe' *always* means Bird's-foot-trefoil in Clare's poetry; but that when he was asked in 1820 to supply a more general English name, he searched in one or other of the popular herbals and gardening books then available to him for a yellow vetch-like flower that grew in grassy places such as the 'balks' dividing an open field, and got hold of the wrong name – or rather, of the two English names, 'Kidney-vetch, Ladies finger', provided in 1660 by John Ray and repeated by many other writers, for the plant that later came to be called *A. vulneraria*. If Bird's-foot-trefoil was in fact what he was looking up, 'lady's finger' may well have conjured up the long tapering seedpods of a plant whose common English name he still did not know. He had however learnt it – in all probability from Henderson – by 1825, when he recorded 'Hornet Moth found feeding on the Birds foot Trefoil in Royce Wood' (NH, 259) – although in this instance the species would not have been *Lotus corniculatus*, but the damp-loving Greater Bird's-foot-trefoil, *L. pedunculatus*.

A three-stress name does not fit easily into metre, and Clare continued to use 'lambtoe' in his poetry in contexts that increasingly suggest that Bird's-foot-trefoil was what he had in mind. In 'Pastoral Fancies', written early in 1828, he speaks of 'The Lambtoe tuft the paler culver key' (MP IV, 414), a line which may contrast the strong yellow, orange and red that have earned Bird's-foot-trefoil the further name of 'eggs-and-bacon' with the lighter tones of Kidney Vetch flowers clustering together like a bunch of keys. If so, this use of 'culver key' appears to be Clare's first and last allusion to the very beautiful Kidney Vetch that has now, because its preferred site is open grassland, become rare in his district. Common Bird's-foot-trefoil, by contrast, has long flourished on farmland and in Clare's day was grown as a fodder crop, although a reference to the seeds of 'trefoil' troubling 'all the land from rig to furrow' ('The leaves of Autumn...', LP, 524) shows it was unwelcome in cornfields. In the summer after his move to Northborough 'plats of lambtoe' in a mown hayfield helped restore his 'Summer Happiness' (MP IV, 314), and in due course lovers in his asylum verse were to walk 'over clumps of lady fingers' ('"Twas in the midst of June...', LP, 718) and 'gather lamb toes in the grass' once the hay harvest was over ('To Julia', LP, 914).

VETCHES, *Vicia* spp.

Clare has some brief allusions in his poems to blue and yellow vetches (which he spells 'fetches'), but our only clues to the species he has in mind come in one of his comments on Elizabeth Kent's *Flora Domestica*: 'there are two most beautiful ones of this kind natives of England one bearing yellow large flowers leafd like an everlasting pea (which also grows wild in our woods) the other is purple or rather dark blue and smaller. They both inhabit hedges and climb like a pea' (NH, 14). In fact the yellow one is a pea and figures in the next entry but one. Of the species suggested by Grainger for Clare's dark blue vetch, Tufted Vetch, *V. cracca*, seems the most likely. The vigorous Bush Vetch, *V. sepium*, could be the one that occurs as 'Heaths creeping fetch' in Clare's poetry (most notably when it crowns his 'Rural Muse' in the poem addressed to her, EP II, 435), though this could equally well be the similarly rampant Common Vetch, *V. sativa*.

Another member of this genus is the Broad Bean, *V. faba*, which is 'the garden beans with flannel lined' gathered and shelled in some lively verses about activities in and around a farm kitchen ('The cowboy shuns the shower...', MP V, 272).

LENTIL, *Lens culinaris*

A passing mention of 'The lintel in the pod' in a late 'Song' ('The bearded rye…', LP, 298) shows that this pulse, which had long been popular as Lenten fare on the Continent, was being grown in Northamptonshire in Clare's lifetime.

PEAS, *Lathyrus* spp.

The yellow vetch described by Clare in the passage quoted above under 'Vetches' is unmistakably Meadow Vetchling, *L. pratensis*; and the species which he says it resembles by having undivided leaves is Narrow-leaved Everlasting-pea, *L. sylvestris*, now rare in the Helpston neighbourhood. Both the cultivated Broad-leaved Everlasting-pea, *L. latifolius*, and the Sweet Pea, *L. odoratus*, figure in gardens in Clare's poetry ('The Cross Roads', EP II, 628; 'Scraps of Tragedy', MP II, 89). In July 1825 he was himself looking forward to receiving 'a curious "Everlasting Pea"' from the Milton Hall garden (NH, 250).

GARDEN PEA, *Pisum sativum*

'Long twining peas in faintly misted greens' ('Sunday Walks' EP II, 645) were a familiar crop in the fields round Helpston. Like beans, they had the additional merit of putting nutrition back into the soil. They also provided much-needed nourishment for Clare himself in his herding days:

> We sought the hollow ash that was shelter from the rain
> With our pockets full of peas we had stolen from the grain
> How delicious was the dinner time on such a showry day
> ('Remembrances', MP IV, 131)

– a 'wild repast' most safely enjoyed on a Sunday when the fields' owners were

> Safe nodding oer their books a church

Or on their benches by the door
Telling their market profits oer
> ('A Sunday with Shepherds and Herdboys', MP II, 17).

RESTHARROWS, *Ononis repens* and *O. spinosa*

Although the name 'restharrow' occurs in poems Clare wrote at
Northampton, he grew up calling these sprawling and sometimes
spiny plants of rough grassland 'finweed', a name that was still in use
in Helpston a century later. Both names relate to their extremely tough
roots. 'Restharrow' is literally 'stop the harrow' and 'finweed' alludes to the
small projections or 'fins' that were designed to prevent plough coulters
becoming clogged in the same way.

Bees, Clare tells us in 'A Morning Walk' (MP III, 354), are attracted
to 'The stinking finweed' by its showy 'pea like flowers', but go away
disappointed. This is explained by the absence of nectaries: it is the leaves
which, when trodden on, do indeed smell – of Vaseline!

CLOVERS, *Trifolium* spp.

White Clover, *T. repens*, and Red Clover, *T. pratense*, bring one of Clare's
best sonnets to its close:

> The herd cows toss the mole hills in their play
> And often stand the strangers steps at bay
> Mid clover blossoms red and tawney white
> Strong scented with the summers warm delight
>> ('The Beans in Blossom', MP IV, 192).

As a one-time herdboy, Clare knew the danger of letting cattle stray into a
clover field, and it provided him with a powerful political simile:

> While they die gorg'd like beast in clover
> We die for wants of bread
>> ('Thy eye can witness…', EP I, 505).

But it is the delights of taste and smell afforded by being 'in clover' that predominate in his poetry, from the early sonnet 'To a Red Clover Blossom' (EP II, 68) onwards. Hares revel in it; clover stacks afford a quickly-snatched treat to a working carthorse or a straying donkey; and the nectar at the bottom of clover 'bottles' – the country word for the individual florets in a head of clover – provides small treats for the human young as well as a vital food for bumble bees. Clover offers another sort of comfort when some trusses of it 'piled up about 6 or more feet square' provide Clare with 'a better bed' than he could have hoped for, on the first night of his journey out of Essex in 1841 (*By Himself*, 258).

LABURNUM, *Laburnum anagyroides*

This ornamental tree, introduced to English gardens in Tudor times, probably grew in the grounds of Northampton Asylum, since it gets a mention in one of Clare's later poems ('The healthfull mind...', LP, 232).

BROOM, *Cytisus scoparius*

The lime-hating Broom was and remains a rare plant in Clare's district. But it could sometimes be found alongside 'Furze brake and mozzling ling' ('June', MP I, 82) in acidic patches of limestone heath, and he knew it well enough to put on record the dazzling colour of its flowers 'That rivals sunshine' ('Pleasures of Spring, MP III, 62), as well as its attractiveness to butterflies: 'the blue and brown skippers / Where jumping and dancing along the gold broom' ('Margaret', LP, 601). Widely known at the time as 'Scotch broom', it recurs often in the Burns-like songs with which Clare filled some of the empty hours of asylum life and which kept up the plant's traditional association with love-making. One song, beginning 'It was a pleasant Evening', goes on to tell us that 'The broom flower was as yellow as a new found rock o' Gold' and ends:

I kissed her i' the green broom i' extacys delight
Then went home to her Cottage and kissed [her] a' the night
(LP, 842).

DYER'S GREENWEED, *Genista tinctoria*

Although the first record of this plant in England is from the site of the battle of Naseby in Northamptonshire in 1788, Clare deserves to be credited with the first record of it in Rutland: 'Found a Species of Broom in Bushy Close of a dwarf kind the like sort grows in great quantitys on Casterton Cowpasture' (NH, 251). He also alludes to 'the dwarf broom' in a late lyric ('To Miss W.....', LP, 415). But there is no indication that he knew of its past importance as a dye-plant, which accounts for the specific adjective *tinctoria*.

GORSES, *Ulex* spp.

Linnaeus is said to have fallen on his knees at his first sight, in England, of Gorse, *U. europaeus* (plate 11). Clare may be recalling this legend – sadly, it is no more than that – when he writes about 'heaths oerspread with furze blooms sunny shine / Where wonder pauses to exclaim "divine"' ('Pleasant Places', MP IV, 225). Certainly gorse, or 'furze' as Clare more usually calls it, when fully in blossom constitutes one of nature's great spectacles, and one which Clare is happy to share with the reader again and again – most dramatically, perhaps, in the command to

> see the rainbow what a stride
> It spands accross the bushy heath
> While furze shine in their golden pride
> A golden ocean underneath
>   ('Birds Nesting', MP II, 175).

The bushy heath was Ailsworth Heath, only three miles south of Helpston but a long walk from Northborough for a man in poor health. Faced with the move, Clare could only resolve to return once a year 'to see the furze in flower on Emmonsails heath' (NH, 318) – perhaps also hoping first to pass over Helpston Heath, where 'The golden furze blooms burnt the wind / With sultry sweets' ('Langley Bush', MP V, 6). By 1836 he was no longer able to return to these haunts and asked Henderson to send him a plant of the compact and double-flowered cultivated variety (*Letters*, 630).

Gorse is not an approachable plant, and in calling it 'unmolested' ('Solitude', EP II, 341) Clare was characteristically thinking that its spines made it a safe refuge from man for other creatures such as rabbits or the linnets which go by the country name of 'furze larks' in his poetry. But in fact it was freely cut by villagers for fuel and might be transplanted to make a fox covert (NH, 226–27); Clare himself dug up bushes of it for his garden (NH, 224, 226).

During his stay at High Beach, Clare encountered a 'furze, like myrtle, scarce a finger long' ('The Botanist's Walk', LP, 36). This was Dwarf Gorse, *U. minor*, which in Britain grows chiefly in the south-east. It appears as 'Dwarf furze' in the 'Child Harold' sequence (LP, 76).

Rose family, ROSACEAE

PEACHES, CHERRIES and PLUMS, *Prunus* spp.

Wild or cultivated, all species of *Prunus* offer spectacular spring blossom followed by fleshy fruits that can be eaten, albeit sometimes with a grimace. The most sweet and succulent is the Peach, *P. persica*, which as its botanical name indicates comes from the warm south. Clare, in one of his first poems, pictures an ideal garden where 'Peach and pear in ruddy lustre glow' against a sunny wall ('The Wish', EP I, 46). At the other end of the edibility scale is Bird Cherry, *P. padus*, not native to the Soke, which Clare may first have seen at Northampton, where he wrote a lilting love lyric that begins 'The bird cherrys white in the dews o' the morning' (LP, 185). Beautiful as are its spires of blossom, its fruit is best left for the birds. The same is true of the Wild Cherry, *P. avium*. Uncommon in the Soke, it appears to come to Clare's poetic notice only when it is bare and stands out by virtue of its colourful bark. Nonetheless, it is the ancestor of the

> black red cherrys shining to the sight
> As rich as brandy held before the light
> ('August', MP I, 127)

grown in orchards and sold in Clare's day on the steps of Helpston's village cross. Moreover, when it comes to the making of cherry brandy, the wild fruit is preferred to its cultivated progeny.

The early flowering of another *Prunus*, Blackthorn, *P. spinosa* (plate 4), takes Clare by surprise according to a sonnet in which its 'snowy blossoms'

> catch the eye
> Like pleasant fancys rising unawares
> – Shining at distance like cloaths hung to drye
> On naked hedges one scarce thinks of flowers
> ('Spring' ['The eldern opens…'], EP II, 583).

Climate change means that the surprise comes even earlier nowadays. But we have stopped eating the sloes which are the Blackthorn's fruit, though they are still the vital ingredient of sloe gin. Helpston children, however, thought these blue-black fruits, once they had been softened by frost, were 'as choice as plumbs' ('Childhood', MP III, 244), and their parents considered 'hissing sputtering sloes' roasted on the branch 'a pleasant treat' ('The Last of Summer', MP II, 53).

The Wild Plum, *P. domestica*, which Clare knew as 'bullace', has a more immediately palatable fruit and is the progenitor of the orchard variety, 'clustering plums … Of freckld red', lusciously described in 'The Last of Summer' (MP II, 52). The 'misty blue' ones in the same passage are Damsons, *P. domestica* ssp. *insititia*, to which Clare makes passing reference in other poems.

CHINESE QUINCE, *Chaenomeles speciosa*

In January 1836 Clare wrote out of deep dejection to Henderson, asking him to send various shrubs for his garden and adding 'my wife also wants a red japonica' (*Letters*, 630). A Chinese Quince (usually called 'japonica'), soon to burst into blossom, would have been a comfort to Patty Clare who, as we know from Clare's publisher's account of his visit around this time, was struggling to keep a home together in the face of her husband's increasing insanity. But Henderson sent only evergreen shrubs in response, so we must assume that even the Milton garden could not furnish a spare plant of what was still an exotic species, first brought to Britain in 1784.

PEAR, *Pyrus communis*

Here and there in Clare's poetry there are mouth-watering allusions to pears, 'so juicy ripe and better still / So rich they een might suck em thro a quill' ('August', MP I, 127). But what are we to make of his observation that pear trees always lean towards the west, which in the Soke is the quarter of the prevailing winds? (NH, 109). Only perhaps that he was uncertain about points of the compass!

APPLES, *Malus* spp.

'Boyhood Pleasures' that Clare, according to a poem with that title, once shared with his friends included stripping the wayside Crab Apple, *M. sylvestris*, of its fruit ('O could I feel...', MP V, 116), which would then be set to 'froth and frizzle' on a makeshift fire ('The Shepherd's Fire', MP IV, 194). But these 'wilding apples', as he calls them (LP, 763) can never have been as sweet and juicy as those he and his companions stole from orchards. Cultivated Apples, *M. pumila*, are the age-old symbol of desirability and Clare's later love songs have plenty of allusions to girls sweet as apple blossom, with cheeks as red as the fruit, and – rather oddly – round-faced like apples.

Apples had more down-to-earth associations for Clare's parents. The crop from an apple tree in their garden was usually large enough to pay their annual rent, but when the tree failed to bear they fell into arrears and his father, already on parish relief, was in danger of removal to the poorhouse (*By Himself*, 117). Before this could happen, however, Clare was 'discovered' as a poet; and when, four years on, the tree again cropped well, Parker Clare sent a gift of its fruit to his son's publishers (*Letters*, 260). They would have enjoyed a taste that we cannot often share today, for these were Golden Russet apples – Shakespeare's 'leather-coats' – not usually considered pretty enough for supermarkets. Nor are most of us ever likely to taste the 'streakd apples suggar sweet' that were called jennetings (Clare's 'Jenitens') because they were held to ripen by St John's night ('August', MP I, 127), or the other early apple known as 'Marigolds' ('Can ye love lowland lassie', LP, 989).

WILD SERVICE-TREE, *Sorbus torminalis*

On 8 March 1825 Clare 'went to Royce wood to get some Service trees to set in Billings Close' (NH, 228). These would not have been seedlings, which are rare, but the suckers by which this marker of ancient woodland, highly valued today for its snowy blossom and brilliant autumn colour, generally reproduces itself. Clare's sonnet, 'The Surry Tree', celebrates not only its beauty but also the distinctive flavour of its fruits, once these have been bletted by frost:

> Tree of the tawny berry rich though wild
> When mellowed to a pulp yet little known
> Though shepherds by its dainty taste beguiled
> Swarm with clasped leg the smooth trunk timber grown
> And pulls the very topmost branches down
> Tis beautiful when all the woods tan brown
> To see thee thronged with berrys ripe and fine
> For daintier palates fitting then the clown
> Where hermits of a day may rove and dine
> Luxuriantly amid thy crimson leaves ...   (MP IV, 329–30).

HAWTHORNS, *Crataegus* spp.

Under its various names of 'thorn', '(h)awthorn', 'whitethorn', 'may' and 'quick', Clare alludes to Hawthorn more often than he does to any other plant, the likeliest reason for this being that no other growing thing attracted his notice more frequently and flamboyantly. It is a plant with three epiphanies. Early in the year, whole hedgerows suddenly break into leaf with 'the green enthusaism of young spring' ('How beautiful the white thorn...', LP, 523). Then, in May, knobbly white buds burst no less suddenly into blossom, an effect that Clare equates with that of poetry when it uses

> A language that is ever green
> That feelings unto all impart
> As awthorn blossoms soon as seen
> Give may to every heart   ('Pastoral Poesy', MP III, 581).

Finally, in the same hedgerows in autumn, 'Awes swarm so thick till bushes seem to burn' ('Fragment', ['The hedge row hips...'], MP V, 58) with a range of reds lovingly described in the essay 'Autumn', written at Northborough in 1841 after the poet's daring escape from his four-year exile in Epping Forest (NH, 330, 333, 335).

These are landscape effects, painted with a broad brush, and though Clare relishes the 'pinky heads / Like fairy pins' of the flowers' stamens ('The Flitting', MP III, 486) he appears not to have noticed that some of the berries which tasted 'like sugar plumbs' to him as a boy ('Remembrances', MP IV, 131) had one seed and others had two. The small thorn trees which he names as part of the woodland understorey in 'Walks in the Woods' (MP III, 571) would have been the two-stoned Midland Hawthorn, *C. laevigata*, which tolerates shade. But the dominant species was and still is the sun-loving *C. monogyna* (plate 7), planted by the million during the early nineteenth century. Despite his hatred of the Enclosures, Clare sometimes had to take casual work planting hedges; the irony of this is underlined by the concern we feel today when these quickset hedges, now sheltering a rich flora and fauna, are grubbed out in the name of efficient land use.

Long before the Enclosures, Hawthorn – either because of its sudden transfigurations or because of Christ's crown of thorns – had acquired religious significance. In particular, the Glastonbury Thorn, *C. monogyna* forma *praecox* (also called 'Biflora'), was considered a holy tree by virtue of its flowering at Christmas time, and Clare imagines it growing in the garden of a past Helpston vicar, the saintly William Paley ('The Parish', EP II, 758, variant reading). This aura of sanctity may have helped to give landmark status to certain thorns even though this is not a dominating tree. Clare several times wrote feelingly about the 'sacred shade' of Langley Bush (EP II, 250) – more generally and properly called Langdyke Bush – which stood on a knoll overlooking Helpston Heath. The site of a medieval open court, its name has appeared for nearly two hundred years on successive editions of the relevant Ordnance Survey map. Since one of Clare's early poems ('The hind that were chopping them up...', EP I, 543–4) records its destruction in a storm, the Langley Bush that was felled by vandals in 1823, as noted in the poet's journal for 1824 (NH, 183), must already have been a replacement. The John Clare Society has had better fortune with the one they planted on the same spot in 1996, now a flourishing tree.

Thrushes sang in Clare's Langley Bush, and he valued 'The blackbird haunted white thorn tree' ('Song – White Thorn Tree', LP, 220) as a refuge for many other kinds of bird including linnets, jays, magpies, chaffinches and wrens. Nesting sites were to be found in the close-woven layering of a quickset hedge or on the stumps of a coppiced woodland hawthorn, this last being much favoured by nightingales. Even the ground under a 'squatting thorn' in what we would call scrub offered a home to nightjars ('The Fern Owl's Nest', MP IV, 300) and the sedge warbler could find a place to build its 'little benty [i.e. grassy] nest' in a thorn bush that was 'So low een grass oer topt its tallest twig' ('Sedge Bird's Nest', MP IV, 153). But Clare's most vivid conjunction of birds and thorn trees is an autumnal one. Towards the end of their long migratory flight across the North Sea and the Wash, flocks of fieldfares would descend on Helpston's haw-laden hedges with cries ('chinnying' is Clare's word for it elsewhere) loud enough to reach the ears of Clare's father inside the barn where he was threshing ('With hand in waistcoat thrust...', MP V, 277).

MEADOWSWEET, *Filipendula ulmaria* (plate 8)

This was Queen Elizabeth I's favourite strewing herb on account of its heady scent; but for Clare two other things distinguish this plant of stream-sides and damp meadows. One is the showiness of its creamy blossoms. In the early poem 'Summer' ('The oak's slow-opening leaf...', EP I, 521), he writes 'The meadow-sweet taunts high its showy wreath' and *Poems Descriptive of Rural Life and Scenery* supplies the gloss 'tosses, as if scornfully', for 'taunt', suggesting a pride such as drought has brought low in 'Noon':

Drowking lies the Meadow sweet   *Drooping*
Flopping down beneath ones feet   (EP I, 406).

The second thing that makes Meadowsweet distinctive for Clare, and that he alludes to in two further poems, is its transformation as wind turns over the plant's dark green 'lappet leaves' and causes them to 'shine all hoary on their under side' ('Rhymes in the Meadows', MP III, 578; 'Nature beautiful every where', MP II, 293).

BRAMBLES, *Rubus* spp.

Blackberries, the fruit of the Bramble, *R. fruticosus* agg., described by Clare as 'rambling bramble berries pulp and sweet / Arching their prickly trails' ('Autumn', ['Syren of sullen moods and fading hues'], MP III, 263), were also called 'mulberries' in his part of the country. They came, he believed, from four distinct kinds of bramble-bush, though he records in his journal entry for 2 January 1825 that his friend Henderson thought there were only two (NH, 213). One could fancifully view this jump from two to four as the beginning of two and a half centuries of exponential increase in botanists' counts of *Rubus* species; by the time Margaret Grainger edited Clare's natural history writing, the total had reached over four hundred (and some experts made it much higher). The explanation is that brambles are for the most part apomictic – that is, they produce seed without fertilisation – so that each small genetic mutation can give rise to a new species.

    Henderson's second kind of bramble was presumably Dewberry, *R. caesius*, which Clare in the early poem 'Autumn' ('The summer flower has run to seed', EP II, 74) had mistakenly called 'mistey blue / Bilberries' (the real Bilberry, *Vaccinium myrtillus*, does not grow in the Soke) but which the same 1825 journal entry rightly names as 'the small creeping "dew berry" that runs along the ground in the land furrows and on the brinks of brooks'. Shortly afterwards it would figure in the dramatic opening of 'The Yellow Hammer's Nest':

Just by the wooden brig a bird flew up
Frit by the cowboy as he scrambled down

To reach the misty dewberry – let us stoop
And seek its nest…
(MP III, 515).

All brambles are painfully thorny, but Clare's sonnet 'The Bramble' (MP IV, 329) ends by praising these much sworn-at plants for the colour they bring to woodland in winter, and elsewhere he writes of the way that their 'weather beaten leaves of purple stain / In hardy stubborness cling all the year' ('A Copse in Winter', EP II, 63). Another early poem, 'The Village Funeral', ends with a description of a new grave marked and protected by bramble branches:

There the grave closes where a mother sleeps
With brambles platted on the tufted grass.   (EP I, 227).

CINQUEFOILS, *Potentilla* spp.

The generic name *Potentilla* tells us that the 'five-fingered weeds' are held to be small but powerful, and their English (or rather, Anglo-French) name 'cinquefoil' points to one reason for this: five was a magical number, 'the symbol at your door' of the folk song 'Green Grow the Rushes-O' being a pentagon. In Clare's time there was much interest in the prevalence of fives in nature, and the last part of 'The Eternity of Nature' (MP III, 531) reflects this: besides the five markings on many flowers and the five-egg clutch laid by many birds, the passage includes 'The five leaved grass trailing its golden cups' – that is, Creeping Cinquefoil, *P. reptans*.

Another species, Tormentil, *P. erecta*, differs from other potentillas in having four, not five, petals. Despite this, it has been held since antiquity to have a magical nature that endows it with curative strength, and it owes its name to its supposed effectiveness against the pains of colic. Along with Creeping Cinquefoil, it has a place in the pharmacopoeia of Clare's Village Doctress:

Tormentil also with its yellow bloom
Thriving on wild uncultivated land

And creeping five leaved grass that maketh room
In every spot its tendrills to expand
These would she gather with right careful hand
And hang them up to dry in many a row...   (MP III, 338).

Gipsies too practised herbal remedies; in his autobiographical writings
Clare says they used Tormentil, which they called 'furze bound', as a cure
for fevers and adder bites (*By Himself*, 85).

Silverweed, *P. anserina*, familiar to Clare as 'spreading goosegrass trailing
all abroad / In leaves of silver green' (MP III, 531), also earns a mention in
'The Eternity of Nature' for its five-petalled flowers. Geese love to gobble
the feathery leaves, which in Clare's day were also tucked inside boots as
a relief for tired, sweaty feet: conveniently for this, one of Silverweed's
habitats is the impacted soil of footpaths.

WILD STRAWBERRY, *Fragaria vesca*

All Clare's strawberries are the wild kind, such as might be found in a
clearing of an oakwood, where blackbirds are nesting in the Hazel
understorey:

Where open spots can meet the sky
Sweet resting places seldom found
Wild strawberries entertain the eye
With crimson berrys shining round
Uncropt unlooked for and unknown
So birds have gardens of their own
          ('Walks in the Woods', MP III, 570).

In other poems, such as 'Careless Rambles', the poet enjoys for himself
'the luscious strawberry ripe and red / As beautys lips' (MP IV, 264), while
in the fantasy world of his late lyrics beauty itself, in the form of 'Lucy',
helps him gather strawberries 'Where the woodbrook moists the mossy
roots of old Oak tree' ('Where the hazels hing...', LP, 851). But the hawk
that hovers overhead is perhaps an ill omen since, in another late poem,

summer, lovers and fruit have all gone:

> Wild strawberry's which both gathered then
> None knows now where they grew
> ('Now is past...', LP, 799).

WOOD AVENS, *Geum urbanum*

Clare deserves to be credited with the first record in his county of this 'common hedgerow plant' (also called Herb Bennet), which in January 1825 he noticed was in leaf in hedgerows to the south of Helpston village (NH, 216). It is in fact winter-green.

AGRIMONY, *Agrimonia eupatoria*

What earns Agrimony a mention in Clare's poetry is not its spike of yellow flowers or its graceful foliage, but its age-old reputation as a curative herb. The Woodman, in a poem of that name, gathers and dries it in summer as a safeguard against winter ailments ('The beating snow...', EP II, 292).

SALAD BURNET, *Poterium sanguisorba*

Bee-haunted and looking 'like little honey combs' ('Rhymes in the Meadows', MP III, 578), the 'burnet buttons' that grow on anthills ('Recollections after a Ramble', EP II, 188) must be those of Salad Burnet, since Great Burnet, *Sanguisorba officinalis*, has longer flower-heads and likes damper soil. Clare several times includes the plant in the flowery setting that he gives to one or other named girl in his later love lyrics.

ROSES, *Rosa* spp.

In June of any year, wild roses are the glory of the hedgerows around Clare's native village. Their splendour helped him bring fresh life to the otherwise tired old association between a young girl's cheeks and the delicate colouring of the Dog-rose, *R. canina* (plate 7):

The wild rose swells its prickly buds anew
And soon shall wear the summers witching hue
Those hues which nature as its dowery heirs
And beauty like a blossom wins and wears
On her soft cheeks when shepherds in the grove
Reach down the blushing flowers and talk of love
The very bees that such intrusions scare
Frit from the blossom that he culls her there
Flye round mistaken as they leave the bower
And take the maids sweet blushes for a flower
Thus wild dog roseys hung in every hedge
Waken at joys hearts core its sweetest pledge
Shedding to summer lanes their rich perfume
And whispering memorys raptures while they bloom (MP IV, 282–3).

Though Clare here makes use of the flower's common name, 'The Flitting' (MP III, 486) shows that he disliked it on account of its 'heedless scorn', and the title he gives the sonnet just quoted is 'The Hedge Rose'. His journal (NH, 213–14) distinguishes between this species and the white-flowered one that is now known as Field-rose, *R. arvensis*, but that he recognised as essentially a woodland-edge plant: the vivid green of its young stems among the tree trunks is one of his 'Pleasures of Spring' (MP III, 53).

Another wayside rose, known today as Harsh Downy-rose, *R. tomentosa*, differs from the Dog-rose by having rough and hairy grey-green leaves instead of glossy ones. Clare found it growing at the south-west corner of Ailsworth Heath, but it was 'not common' (NH, 78), and indeed is classed as 'uncommon' in today's floras. On the other hand, he noted that Sweet-briar, *R. rubiginosa*, which differs from other roses in an extreme prickliness and an apple-like scent 'as sweet as child's breath' ('The Sweet-briar', LP, 665), grew 'wild in plenty about our heaths' (NH, 21). Today it is something of a rarity in the district, as is its close relation, Small-flowered Sweet-briar, *R. micrantha*, which Clare calls 'a sort of bastard sweetbrier' (NH, 21) and which prefers scrub or woodland to an open site. Castor Hanglands is one place where both sweet-briars can still be found.

In addition to these five species of native rose, Clare was familiar with various introduced roses, though the range of these was small compared with what it is today. He must have come across Damask Roses, R. × *damascena*, while he was still learning his job as a gardener: they appear in the very early poem, 'The Wish' (EP I, 47). Later on, his journal and letters show him eager to acquire, from a gardening friend who lived near London, a sucker of the 'White Province Rose' (NH, 227; *Letters*, 320, 327, 330); this would have been the Great White Rose of York, R. × *alba*, thought by some to have been a cross, originating in Provence, between the Dog-rose and the Damask Rose. Despite 'fine province roses' and 'fine cabbage roses' being manuscript variants in the June section of *The Shepherd's Calendar* (MP I, 81), they were two distinct species to Clare, who pictures a many-petalled Cabbage (or Moss) Rose, R. × *centifolia* 'Muscosa', thrusting through a garden fence to tempt a passing child ('The blooms all fragrant...', MP II, 104).

All these old European roses bloom only once a year, around midsummer; but in the late eighteenth century China Roses, praised by Clare in his journal for their repeated flowering (NH, 203), were introduced from the Far East. If the climbing rose that Henderson promised to give Clare in 1825 (NH, 250) lived to be 'The Evergreen Rose' that he wrote a poem about seven years later, it cannot just have been the European climber R. *sempervirens* but must have had some oriental ancestry, since it bore 'roseys all the year' – causing the wren to cock its tail and whistle in amazement (MP III, 537).

Buckthorn family, RHAMNACEAE

ALDER BUCKTHORN, *Frangula alnus*

On 16 March 1825, Clare recorded in his journal that he went to Oxey Wood and dug up 'a stoven of Black alder to set in my garden' (NH, 230) – an entry that must make any conservationist wince, for 'black alder' or Alder Buckthorn, the '*Alnus nigra*' of early herbals, though it has been recorded in other woods near Helpston in the past, has always been very rare in the Soke. This said, a specimen would certainly have enhanced Clare's garden; a slender and thornless small tree, it has leaves that feed

64

caterpillars of the brimstone butterfly in summer and turn bright yellow in autumn, and berries that progress from green to red to dark purple. Clare probably knew too that these berries would furnish a milder laxative than did the ferociously named *Rhamnus cathartica*, the common Buckthorn (sometimes called 'purging buckthorn').

Another brief allusion in Clare's prose writings to 'the alder black and spotted like the hazel' (NH, 31) explains how he was able to identify a leafless sapling of *F. alnus*: Alder Buckthorn twigs are covered with the conspicuous warty spots called lenticels. A further mention of 'black alder' is however to the dark bole of the 'true' Alder, *Alnus glutinosa*: see p. 72.

Elm family, ULMACEAE

ELMS, *Ulmus* spp.

In Clare's day the Wych Elm, *U. glabra*, was already recognised by its broader boughs and larger leaves as a different species from the English Elm, *U. procera*. His own usage suggests however that he made no such distinction, but thought of 'whychen' or 'whichen' as an alternative name for elm.

An elm tree that had long sheltered Clare's family home was cut down in 1830. The event prompted him to write 'The Fallen Elm', a great outburst of anger against landlords who believed they could do what they liked with their own. In 1976 I thought I was re-living Clare's situation when I bought a small cottage beside a huge elm, only to discover on moving in that agents of the ground landlord, who happened to be the Duke of Marlborough, had felled the tree. But there was one big difference. 'My' elm was blighted by Dutch elm disease, so the Duke had no choice in the matter. Indeed we were fellow-victims, he having lost at Blenheim Palace whole battalions of elms drawn up in the battle order of his forebear's victory. The ravages of this disease in the last century, followed by the wholesale elimination of the hedgerows of which elms had been the chief feature, has changed the look of lowland England for ever. Now only elderly people can remember the elm's dark strength, that density of timber and foliage which Clare celebrates in several poems, but nowhere better than in 'The Fallen Elm':

Old favourite tree thoust seen times changes lower
Though change till now did never injure thee
For time beheld thee as her sacred dower
And nature claimed thee her domestic tree
Storms came and shook thee many a weary hour
Yet stedfast to thy home thy roots hath been
Summers of thirst parched round thy homely bower
Till earth grew iron – still thy leaves was green
The childern sought thee in thy summer shade
And made their play house rings of sticks and stone
The mavis sang and felt himself alone
While in thy leaves his early nest was made
And I did feel his happiness mine own
Nought heeding that our friendship was betrayed.

(MP III, 441).

Hop family, CANNABACEAE

HOP, *Humulus lupulus*

In 'Flower gathering' (MP II, 103) Clare writes about hedgerows where wild Hops 'lift in rambling rout / Their clammy balls of fruit' – 'clammy' because, as Richard Mabey explains, 'Each lobe of the cone-like structure is studded near its base with yellow glands, which exude a mixture of aromatic oils and resins known as lupulin.' It was this substance, source of the bittering agent in beer, that accounted for hop gardens being found throughout lowland England in Clare's day.

Nettle family, URTICACEAE

NETTLES, *Urtica* spp.

The nitrogen-hungry Common Nettle, *U. dioica*, which Clare sometimes calls 'the keen nettle' to distinguish it from so-called dead-nettles, thrives in almost any human settlement where neglect gives it its head. One such settlement is the lost village of Pickworth, some ten miles from Helpston, whose inhabitants are thought to have fled from or succumbed to the Black Death. Clare worked there in 1818, making a lime kiln, and the desolate scene where nettles grew 'in triumph oer each heap that swells the ground' inspired his 'Elegy Hastily Composed and Written with a Pencil on the Spot in the Ruins of Pickworth Rutland' (EP I, 403). In the metre and manner of Gray's *Elegy*, this is a deeply melancholy poem in which the still unpublished poet resigns himself to sharing the oblivion of those whose bones he has disturbed in his digging.

In several of the verse tales that Clare planned to accompany *The Shepherd's Calendar*, nettles conform to a rather tired poetic convention, as they invade abandoned gardens or spread on neglected graves. But in the asylum poems he reverts to nettles as he actually remembered them from his labouring and courting days, yellow roots and all ('Boys and Spring', LP, 560): standing 'angrily and dun' ('Spring' ['The sweet spring now is come'ng'], LP, 172), yet 'so richly green' ('My bonny Jane', LP, 746). Their rapid growth covers unused farm implements and makes them part of 'the harmony of Spring' ('Tall grows the nettle...', LP, 186), so that a rural lover can even declare

I love at my labour each bunch o' keen nettles
That grow where I work as the finest o' flowers
                    ('In the Field, LP, 839).

No one could love the ferocious Roman Nettle, *U. pilulifera*, now extinct except as a casual. But in the eighteenth century, according to Philip Miller in *The Gardener's Dictionary* (1741), a cultivated variety of it with leaves that he describes as similar to those of pellitory was grown for practical jokers to insert in bunches of flowers. This plant, rather than the explosive yellow-flowered Touch-me-not Balsam, *Impatiens noli-tangere*, as it is usually explained, must be what Clare means in these lines from 'The Sorrows of Love':

The "touchmenot" that like a nettle stung
What ere it met was often hid among

The flowers of those who lovd rude jokes to trye
Wi fond unthinking wenches passing bye
Offering wi serious face as all were well
Which bit their noses when they bent to smell   (MP I, 168).

Those who 'lovd rude jokes' included the members of a Cambridge college, to judge by the survival in their garden of this variant – the leaves of which, incidentally, are more like those of basil than of pellitory.

PELLITORY-OF-THE-WALL, *Parietaria judaica*

In a poem about his schooldays in the vestry of Glinton church, Clare remembers Ash and Sycamore trees round the churchyard, celandines on the graves, 'And the spire where pelitory dangled and grew' ('Childhood', LP, 651). The last were probably the same plants that, in writing the early poem called 'Solitude', his youthful imagination transferred to a ruined abbey (EP II, 338).

Beech family, FAGACEAE

BEECH, *Fagus sylvatica*

There are no Beech woods in Clare's countryside and so it is only the odd planted tree or group of trees that earns a passing mention in poems he wrote at Helpston and Northborough. But in 1837 he was persuaded to enter Matthew Allen's private asylum at High Beech (now 'Beach') in Epping Forest in Essex, where Beech was the dominant species. 'I loved the Forest walks and beechen woods' he wrote in a sonnet ('A Walk in High Beach, Loughton', LP, 27) dating from the time when, under Allen's humane regime, he was free to roam, his ear alert for the nightingale:

I hear her in the Forest Beach
    When beautiful and new;
Where cow-boys hunt the glossy leaf...
        ('To the Nightingale', LP, 16).

This last line is a reminder that Epping Forest was wood-pasture, where commoners had the right to graze their cattle and lop the trees for firewood; the Beeches thus stood in Clare's eyes for the rights of the poor that were elsewhere overridden by the Enclosure Acts. But the distant view of London, though no more than 'a guess among the trees' (LP, 27) reminded him of the power of riches, and the unrhymed sonnet that on publication was given the title 'London *versus* Epping Forest' (LP, 28) concludes

> I could not bear to see the tearing plough
> Root up and steal the Forest from the poor,
> But leave to freedom all she loves, untamed,
> The Forest walk enjoyed and loved by all!

Time has brought a triple irony to these lines. It was in fact to save the Forest from encroaching enclosure by local landowners that the Corporation of London in 1878 acquired the freehold by Act of Parliament. The same Act, however, decreed on aesthetic grounds that there was to be no more pollarding: as a result the canopy closed and pasturing became impossible. And lastly, Clare himself was destined not to regain real freedom. In July 1841 he walked home from High Beach to Northborough, only to be removed to Northampton General Asylum by the end of the year.

SWEET CHESTNUT, *Castanea sativa*

This tree, probably introduced in Roman times and widely naturalised in most of Britain, was and is uncommon in Clare's home territory, though he may have come across it in Burghley Park, where many Sweet Chestnuts were planted in the eighteenth century. He certainly encountered it in the grounds of Northampton Asylum, in an area he calls 'The Nursery Garden' (LP, 926); and another poem close in time to the one with that title begins 'Sweet chesnuts brown, like soleing leather turn' ('The Winter's Come', LP, 928).

PEDUNCULATE OAK, *Quercus robur* (plate 4)

Oaks of all shapes and sizes are almost as plentiful as Primroses in Clare's poetry. Specimen trees grew to their full magnificence in Burghley Park, and the poet remembered those 'sweet spreading oaks' all his life ('Where the deer with their shadows...', LP, 1107). At the other extreme were the 'pulpit trees' or 'dottrells', this last word being glossed by Clare as 'Old stumping trees in hedge-rows, that are headed every ten or twelve years for fire-wood' (MP V, 662). Straight, tall standards, planted for timber, could be found in the managed woods close to the village; 'The Holiday Walk' (MP III, 406) takes Clare and his children past felled oak trunks already stripped of their bark for tannin. And in the open country to the south and west lay patches of wildwood where immensely old trees with huge and often hollow boles were abundant.

In all these habitats, Clare was fascinated, as D. H. Lawrence would have been, by the 'rich brown-umber hue' of unfolding oak leaves: 'this one tint of natures pencil', he wrote, 'gave me from a boy such a luxu[r]y of happiness that I never could describe it my heart has often ached with the extasty to paint it' (NH, 317–18). In due season he recorded, in verse or prose, the oak's flowering, when 'little green shaggy trails' that were the male flowers appeared alongside 'little red knots' that would become acorns (NH, 108); the stubbornness of oaks in staying green longer than other trees; and the richness of a leaf litter that sheltered the next spring's violets and Primroses and supplied nesting material for chiffchaffs, goldcrests and nightingales. It is a fact that no other tree in Britain gives more hospitality to other forms of life, and the guest list in Clare's poetry is an impressive one: lichens, mosses, ivy, grub-hunting woodpeckers –

In hardest oaks their whimbles go
And dust like sawdust lies below
('Walks in the Woods', MP III, 570)

– as well as nest-building blackbirds and magpies; squirrels that 'sputter up the powdered oak' ('First Sight of Spring', MP IV, 296) and badgers that make their setts in the arching shelter of its roots; the village's pigs let loose for their annual orgy of rootling; and finally their owners, who find 'a happy seat' on the low-slung branches of what the poet calls a 'squatting oak' ('Stray Walks', MP IV, 302).

But Clare's pleasure in the beauty of particular trees was far from secure, for between 1813 and 1816 the Enclosers felled many of Helpston's ancient oaks:

> By Langley bush I roam but the bush hath left its hill
> On cowper green I stray tis a desert strange and chill
> And spreading lea close oak ere decay had penned its will
> To the axe of the spoiler and self interest fell a prey
> And cross berry way and old round oaks narrow lane
> With its hollow trees like pulpits I shall never see again
> Inclosure like a Buonaparte let not a thing remain
> It levelled every bush and tree and levelled every hill
> And hung the moles for traitors – though the brook is running still
> It runs a nake[d] brook cold and chill
> ('Remembrances', MP IV, 133).

Here the long stanza, with its triple metre and dying fall, pulsates with Clare's regret for a vanished landscape. Another locally famous oak did however survive, and inspired a poem that in its colloquial directness and its ecological awareness of the interaction between different forms of life – in this case, man, bird and tree – is even more typical of the poet's responses to the natural world. It describes how a pair of ravens have built their nest in what Clare elsewhere calls 'a large inaccessible oak in Oxey wood' (NH, 127):

> And boys to reach it try all sorts of schemes
> But not a twig to reach with hand or foot
> Sprouts from the pillared trunk and as to try
> To swarm the massy bulk tis all in vain
> They scarce one effort make to hitch them up
> But down they sluther soon as ere they try.

So the birds – firmly believed to be the original pair – are unmolested, the tree remains inviolate, and the poem can end with a moving celebration of continuity and renewal:

> every spring
> Finds the two ancient birds at their old task
> Repairing the hugh nest – where still they live   *huge*
> Through changes winds and storms and are secure
> And like a landmark in the chronicles
> Of village memorys treasured up yet lives
> The hugh old oak that wears the ravens nest
> ('The Raven's Nest', MP III, 559–61).

Walnut family, JUGLANDACEAE

WALNUT, *Juglans regia*

In his journal Clare recalls that a tree grown from a nut that old Will Tyers of Glinton picked up as a boy provided great quantities of nuts before it was cut down and its timber sold for £50 – a lot of money in 1824 (NH, 209). The entry sums up a productivity that has caused the Walnut to be widely planted ever since the Romans brought it to Britain.

In Clare's poetry, two particular Walnut trees are charged with associations. One was in Glinton churchyard, where its low branches swept across the burial place of the man who had taught Clare at the vestry school in Glinton; an early poem, 'To the Memory of James Merrishaw, A Village Schoolmaster' (EP I, 55–6), begins with a passionate protest that the grave remains unmarked. The nut that Clare as a child once threw at Mary Joyce could have come from this tree; he never forgot her tears (*By Himself*, 88), and many years later, as he looked at 'the beautifull Spire of Glinton Church, towering high over the grey willows and dark wallnuts still lingering in the church yard' (NH, 332), he was to write

> Dull must that being live who sees unmoved
> The scenes and objects that his childhood knew

The school yard and the maid he early loved
The sunny wall where long the old Elms grew
The grass that e'en till noon retains the dew
Beneath the wallnut shade I see them still …

('Child Harold', LP, 62).

But at this point in the poem the Glinton Walnut merges with another in the garden of Clare's birthplace, and it is this Walnut tree that makes its presence felt throughout the poet's 1824–25 journal. Departing swallows gather in it in September; it is bare by late October; sparrows nest in it in February; it breaks into new leaf in April, sheds its catkins in May, and then in June – casting a shadow of the future – 'the Baloon with Mr Green and Miss Stocks' passes directly over it (NH, 248).

Birch Family, BETULACEAE

SILVER BIRCH, *Betula pendula*

This beautiful tree appears to have been far less frequent in the Soke in Clare's time than it is today and both his passing allusions to it in his verse occur in poems he wrote at Northampton ('The Autumn Wind', LP, 489; 'The Winter's Come', LP, 929). In one sense, though, he did write on it at Helpston: having learnt, perhaps from Gerard's *Herbal*, that thin layers of white birch bark could serve as a substitute for paper – of which he was often chronically short – he was pleased to discover that 'it recieves the ink very readily' (NH, 220).

ALDER, *Alnus glutinosa*

The distinctively black bark of this moisture-loving, stream-side tree is mentioned by Clare in one of his Natural History Letters (NH, 46). In his day its timber provided piles for fenland buildings, and its bark furnished a black dye and a tannin agent. But recent reclamation of wetland in his area has resulted in its Alders now being virtually confined to the banks of the Welland.

HORNBEAM, *Carpinus betulus*

A tree of south-east England, the Hornbeam remains uncommon in Clare's countryside. In Epping Forest, by contrast, Hornbeams grow by the thousand; hence their appearance in a stanza of 'Child Harold', the disturbed but powerful sequence that Clare wrote in the year he escaped from Dr Matthew Allen's asylum:

How beautiful this hill of fern swells on
So beautifull the chappel peeps between
The hornbeams – with its simple bell – alone
I wander here hid in a palace green
Mary is abscent – but the forest queen
Nature is with me – morning noon and gloaming
I write my poems in these paths unseen
And when among these brakes and beeches roaming
I sigh for truth and home and love and woman   (LP, 46).

HAZEL, *Corylus avellana*

'Dead leaves of ash and oak and hazel tree', Clare records in 'The Wild-flower Nosegay' are 'The constant covering of all woody land' (EP II, 410), and in poem after poem he recreates this well-defined type of woodland, with its tall timber trees, its understorey of hazel and its ground layer of Primroses and Bluebells in spring. Hazels were coppiced for a wonderfully pliant wood that had a multitude of uses, including the making of 'hazel bands' ('January', MP I, 11) to bind faggots of firewood. After each coppicing, the stools (which Clare more usually calls 'stulps', 'stumps' or 'stovens') spread, and in time would make mossy building sites for low-nesting birds such as woodlarks and robins ('The Wood lark's Nest', MP IV, 322; 'The Autumn Robin', MP III, 293), while the whippy new stems, their bark now bearing 'brighter freckles' (the botanists' 'lenticels' – 'Pleasures of Spring', MP III, 53), offered support for twining 'woodbine' and Black Bryony ('Come darling summer', EP II, 41; 'A Morning Walk', EP I, 495) as well as singing-perches for thrushes and nightingales ('A Wish', LP, 640;

'The Nightingale', LP, 461). Clare believed that at the time when 'cats-and-kitlings', as Helpston children called Hazel catkins, first appeared, thrushes began to sing, and that they started to build their nests when the 'female flowers put forth their little crimson threads at the ends of the buds to receive the impregning dust of the male dangling trails' (NH 226; cf. 'First Sight of Spring', MP IV, 296).

On 13 March 1825, Clare 'took a walk to open copy [wood] to see the Nutt trees in flower which promise a great nutting season' (NH, 229), thus reminding us that Hazels were also a valuable source of food. To judge from 'Nutters' (MP IV, 334) – a piece of rough rhyming, the content of which offers a fascinating contrast to Wordsworth's 'Nutting' – the October Hazel harvest was a lively crowd event. Clare however comes close to a Wordsworthian mood in his own 'Nutting', where he appears (as in a poem of the same title written a decade earlier) to have a single companion:

> We left the wood and on the velvet bank
> Of short sward pasture ground we sat us down
> To shell our nutts before we reached the town
> The near hand stubble field with mellow glower
> Showed the dim blaze of poppys still in flower
> And sweet the molehills smelt we sat upon
> And now the thymes in bloom but where is pleasure gone
> (MP IV, 210–11).

Clare of course had many reflective wanderings on his own through Hazel coppices, admiring the 'crimpled sheen' ('Come lovely Mary', LP, 1075) of their leaves. These would turn 'blood red' ('The Milkmaid', LP, 631) in autumn, but he best remembered them in their broad-ribbed summer strength that could support a dragonfly ('Summer' ['How sweet when weary…'], EP II, 56). 'I miss the hazel's happy green' sums up all his regret at having to leave well-wooded Helpston for fen-side Northborough in 1832 ('The Flitting', MP III, 479).

White Bryony family, CUCURBITACEAE

WHITE BRYONY, *Bryonia dioica*

This is unrelated to Black Bryony (see p. 162), though both are hedgerow climbers with red berries. But White Bryony, in addition to the advantage of tendrils to clamber by, has more noticeable flowers and its leaves have five pointed lobes:

Theres another sort still that field hedges adorn
The edge of whose leaves look as tho they were torn
That beareth rude flowers of a pale yellow green
And like the wild hop on most hedges is seen
('A Walk in the Fields', MP III, 389).

If Clare's voice is here a shade instructive, the reason is that he is writing in anticipation of showing the beauties of Helpston's hedges to his London friend Eliza Emmerson.

CUCUMBER and MELON, *Cucumis* spp.

'Written an Essay to day "on the sexual system of plants"', Clare records in his journal for 11 September 1824 (NH, 175). The essay, actually a long note in a manuscript that contains a great deal of Clare's natural history writing, is limited to observations on plants that have distinct male and female flowers. It begins with those such as Melon, *C. melo*, and Cucumber, *C. sativus*, which today are called monoecious (i.e. sharing one house) because there are separate male and female flowers on the same plant.

PUMPKIN, *Cucurbita maxima*

In the cottage garden of 'The Cross Roads', which the story's narrator remembers as a characteristic mixture of the colourful and the useful, 'pumkins neath the window usd to climb' (EP II, 628).

Spindle family, CELASTRACEAE

SPINDLE, *Euonymus europaeus*

> The dog tree squares of green sweeing wi berrys
> Of a glossy pink and foul rice sprigs
> red as bird claws   ('Oft at this leafless season...', MP II, 10).

In these rough notes for a poem the 'dog tree' with distinctively square green stems and pink berries can only be the Spindle, and it is the shrub here called 'foul rice' that normally goes by the name of 'dogwood'. 'Dog' has been taken to be a term of contempt in both names; but who could feel contempt for a shrub with blood-red autumn foliage that Druce calls 'an ornament to our countryside', or for Spindle with berries that Clare describes as 'Glittering and pink as blossoms washed in dew' ('The Spindle Tree', MP IV, 330)? In both names 'dog' in fact implies the use of the wood for *dags*, or skewers, just as the more common English name for *E. europaeus* reminds us that many village housewives of the time would have owned a spindle made from its hard yellow wood.

Spurge family, EUPHORBIACEAE

DOG'S MERCURY, *Mercurialis perennis*

One of the 'Morning Pleasures' of boyhood, as recorded by Clare, is to

> gather cuckoos from the neighbouring lawn
> Where mid the dark Dog mercury that abounds
> Round each mossed stump the woodlark hides her nest
> And delicate bluebell that her home surrounds
> Bows its soft fragrance oer her spotted breast
> Till from the boys rude steps she startled flies
> Who turns the weeds away and vainly seeks the prize
> (MP IV, 215).

A 'lawn' is a woodland glade or ride, where the strongly invasive and shade-loving Dog's Mercury would form thick ground cover round the boles of the trees but would leave the sunnier patches to Early-purple Orchids and Bluebells, in comparison with which it is indeed a mere 'weed'. Predatory boy and all, the lines are a beautifully compact bit of woodland ecology.

CAPER SPURGE, *Euphorbia lathyris*

In his wanderings through Epping Forest, Clare observed both Dog's Mercury and its much less common relative, Caper Spurge – which, he adds, was called 'wild capers' where he came from ('The Botanist's Walk', LP, 36). This tall and handsome plant could conceivably have been a native in either area, but as such it is very rare indeed, so the probability in both cases is that it was of garden origin. Gardeners, however, regard it as a weed, and a danger to children because its fruits resemble edible capers: so how did they come by it in the first place? One answer is that in the past it was believed to keep away moles; another, that Caper Spurge plants found in Clare's day or our own can be the relics of those grown centuries ago for their medicinal properties: Chaucer, for example, knew the plant's power as a laxative.

Passionflower family, PASSIFLORACEAE

PASSIONFLOWERS, *Passiflora* spp.

The Passion flower and Ceres fine
By wealth and pride are reared alone
Yet flowers more sweet nor less divine
Springs humbler fields and forrests own

– and so it is a wreath of wild flowers that Clare puts together for Eliza Emmerson in 'To —— on May Morning' (MP III, 280). The Night-blowing Cereus was a hothouse rarity of the time, and it is unlikely Clare ever saw it. But species of passionflower, though also of tropical origin, had been grown in English gardens for over two hundred years. The reason that Clare associates both with wealth and pride is, I think, because both are depicted in Robert Thornton's *Garden of Flora* (1799–1807), the most magnificent florilegium ever published in England. Clare may have seen a copy or a set of the plates during his stay at the Emmersons' home in London.

Willow family, SALICACEAE

POPLARS, *Populus* spp.

The Aspen, *P. tremula*, which is a native poplar, is rare in Clare country, and Druce decided that the aspen leaves which in 'Summer Images' (MP III, 155) 'Turn up their silver lining to the sun', and make a 'brustling noise' that causes the shepherd boy to run for shelter, in fact belonged to the rather more frequent Grey Poplar, *P.* × *canescens*, which is a hybrid between the Aspen and the introduced White Poplar, *P. alba*. But though this probably is the tree that Clare means when he writes

> The poplar tree it turns to gray
>   As leaves lift up their underside
>   ('The Autumn Wind', LP, 489)

I am inclined to accept his 'aspens' for what they should be and moreover to identify two of his 'poplars' as Aspens – one being the 'small leav'd Poplar' in 'A Rhapsody' (LP, 994) that, 'when all leaves are still / Trembles wi' Ague', and the other in 'Spring' ('How beautiful the spring'), where 'the poplars twittering leafy tide / All wild and hoary on their under side' (MP III, 39) evokes both the sight and sound of breaking waves.

The one time Clare writes of a 'white poplar' it is 'peeping above the rest like leafy steeples' (*By Himself*, 38) – which is less suggestive of *P. alba* than of the Lombardy-poplar, *P. nigra* 'Italica'. For a tree introduced into Britain as recently as 1758, the Lombardy-poplar quickly made itself at home, to the extent that the word 'poplar' soon began to summon up images of something very thin and tall. So the recipients of such late Valentine-style verses as 'My Peggy's a young thing' (LP, 564) were presumably pleased to be told they were slim as poplars; and Clare comes quite naturally to use the dialect word for 'poplars' when what he has in mind are

> The popples tapering to their tops
> That in the blue sky thinly wires
> Like so many leafy spires
>   ('A Sunday with Shepherds and Herdboys', MP II, 16).

WILLOWS, *Salix* spp.

Clare distinguished several kinds of willow. He knew that 'a dwarf willow' (Creeping Willow, *S. repens*) grew in the Fens south of Peterborough, as it does today, and since this has been considered to be a distinct variety, *S. repens* var. *fusca*, he may have been right in claiming it (NH, 62) as special to his area. After his move to Northborough he asked Henderson to send him a sketch of the 'drooping willow in the Island pond' in Milton Hall grounds and, if possible, an actual specimen for his new garden (*Letters*, 627). This would have been the Weeping Willow, *S.* × *sepulcralis*, a garden hybrid between the native White Willow, *S. alba*, and the original Weeping Willow from China, *S. babylonica*. Exploring the fenland landscape around his new home, Clare was grateful for the brilliant stem colour of a third species, the Osier, *S. viminalis*. In 'A Walk', 'little woods / Of osiers made the wilderness be gay' (MP IV, 312), and in 'Child Harold', 'Bright yellow is the osier hedge / Beside the brimming drains' (LP, 71). 'Woods' and 'hedge' suggest Osiers deliberately planted for the long straight stems from which baskets were woven.

    Osiers have narrow leaves, whereas other bushy willows have oval leaves and are generally known as 'sallows', the name 'willow' being kept for substantial trees with narrow leaves and catkins that are curved, unlike the stubby ones of sallows. By and large, Clare observes these distinctions. Occasionally he calls a tree willow a 'sallow', but normally for him sallows mean the bushes that provide the 'palms' for Palm Sunday: bearers, that is, of fat downy catkins that 'Turn like the sunshine into golden light' as the pollen breaks from their anthers ('The March Nightingale', MP IV, 185). The commonest sallow, Grey Willow, *S. cinerea*, likes to be by water, whereas the very similar Goat Willow, *S. caprea*, is more of a woodland plant. The opening lines of 'The Sallow' could thus be said to embrace both species, though I doubt that Clare was distinguishing them as he wrote:

> Pendant oer rude old ponds or leaning oer
> The woodlands mossy rails – the sallows now
> Put on their golden liveries and restore
> The spring to splendid memories ere a bough
> Of white thorn shows a leaf to say tis come
> And through the leafless underwood rich stains
> Of sunny gold show where the sallows bloom
> Like sunshine in dark places and gold veins
> Mapping the russet landscape into smiles
> At springs approach...   (MP IV, 248–9).

S. cinerea is nowadays englished as Grey Willow, but Clare's many allusions to 'grey' willow foliage generally refer to the long, fluttering, silver-backed leaves of tree willows such as the ones that in 'Child Harold' he describes as 'towering' (LP, 70). Once again those he has in mind are likely to be of two species, though he does not himself distinguish between them: the White Willow, *S. alba*, and the Crack Willow, recently renamed the Hybrid Crack-willow, *S. × fragilis*. Both are still abundant in Clare country. The dense foliage of 'The Old Willow' (MP IV, 268) that leaves the poet and his book 'uninjured from the fragrant rain' could well belong to a White Willow, while in 'To Anna Three Years Old', the description of a

> danger daring willow tree
> Who leans an ancient invalid
> Oer spots where deepest waters be   (MP II, 144)

suggests a typically split and contorted Crack Willow, with roots that – to quote 'The Moorhen's Nest' – 'Crankle and spread and strike beneath the flood' (MP III, 471).

What *is* certain is that Clare loved both willows and sallows and that they inspired some of his most memorable poems. This is not surprising when we recall how marked a feature they were of the fenland landscape, veined as it was with willow-bordered streams and scored by pollard-fringed dykes: a landscape Clare readily recognised in the 'rushy flats befringed with willow tree' of Peter De Wint's paintings ('To De Wint', MP IV, 198). Anger at the way the Enclosers ruined these features by straightening watercourses and clearing their banks of vegetation prompted the young Clare to write the highly original 'Lamentations of Round-Oak Waters' –

> O then what trees my banks did crown
>   What Willows flourished here
> Hard as the ax that Cut them down
>   The senceless wretches were   (EP I, 233)

– and to follow them up with a sustained and eloquent protest from 'The Village Minstrel', Lubin, at the desolation caused 'When ploughs destroyd the green when groves of willows fell' (EP II, 168). Lubin's distress at the consequent disappearance of many birds reminds us that one reason why willows meant so much to Clare was that they were essentially habitat trees: their young shoots were pecked by the whitethroats that he knew as 'willow-biters', their branches afforded sunny perches from which 'King fishers watch the ripple stream / For little fish that nimble by' ('Wandering by the rivers edge', MP V, 27), and their roots stretched into the water to make ideal nesting sites for moorfowl.

Violet family, VIOLACEAE

VIOLETS and PANSIES, *Viola* spp.

There are violets by the dozen – a dozen dozen, in fact – in Clare's poetry. They even spring up in his biblical paraphrases: amethysts in the walls of the New Jerusalem are 'blue / As violets that in the old fallen world grew' (LP, 154), and in his imitation of the 148th Psalm the violet's colour proclaims the artistry of God ('Song of Praise', EP II, 604). The sight of that intense colour set off by a glimpse of golden stamens constitutes

Clare's primary experience of violets. He does not trouble to distinguish between the various species that grew abundantly in his neighbourhood as they still do today: some of his allusions may be to remembered clumps of Common Dog-violet, *V. riviniana*, or Early Dog-violet, *V. reichenbachiana*, or Hairy Violet, *V. hirta*. But though 'many sorts are known'

> the sweetest yet that grows
> Is that which every hedgrow owns
> And every body knows
> > ('On seeing some moss…', MP III, 566)

– where 'sweetest' points to the Sweet Violet, *V. odorata*.

Violets come into their own in several of the poems transcribed by William Knight, a member of the Northampton Asylum staff, in which the imagery can be slightly off-beat yet strangely effective, as when Clare describes the happiness of being left free to wander, talking to himself, through woods 'Where the violets melt blue' ('The Humble Bee', LP, 686). Two poems with the title 'Spring Violets' represent the two main types of lyric that Clare wrote during these Northampton years. One is a graceful celebration of flowers 'So purely white so sweetly blue' that grow in 'the sunniest and the sweetest places' (LP, 427–8). It is album verse and its appearance over Clare's signature in an actual album belonging to a Northampton woman suggests that, like many other poems of this period in his life, it was written on request and possibly for a small payment. The other poem (LP, 307–8) by contrast shares with us an epiphanous moment as, with the command 'Push that rough maple bush aside', the poet reveals to us flowers that have only a short time in which to blossom before the woodland canopy closes:

> In their dead leafy beds, how intensely dark blue,
> By the moss maple stump, where the sunshine looks through:
> Those sweet flowers that look up, in their beautiful bloom,
> Will ne'er live to see the bright maple leaves come.

This syndrome of discovery and loss recurs in many of these more personal lyrics, and nowhere more movingly than in the 'Stanzas' beginning 'The spring is come forth, but no spring is for me / Like the spring of my boyhood' (LP, 394–5). Violets are scenting the air in the 'strange woods' where he now finds himself,

> But the wild flowers that bring me most joy and content
> Are the blossoms that blow where my childhood was spent

– flowers that he once gathered in places where he is now scarcely remembered:

> But the violets are there by the dyke and the dell,
> Where I played 'hen and chickens' – and heard the church bell
> Which called me to prayer-book and sermons in vain
> O when shall I see my own vallies again?

Two other members of the genus *Viola* occur in Clare's writings. One is the parti-coloured Garden Pansy, *V.* × *wittrockiana*, also known as 'heartsease', a name that he plays upon whenever he uses it:

> Love may languish in its anguish
> Pansies they are happy beaux
> Sun or rain they feel no pain
> Ever in their sunday cloaths   ('The Pansy', LP, 603).

Clare seems not to have come across the Wild Pansy, *V. tricolor*, which is extremely rare in the Soke, but he knew the yellow Field Pansy, *V. arvensis*, and tried to cultivate it in the hope that it would get bigger – 'but it lovd its wild state so well that it was too stubbon for me and I gave it up to its fields agen' (NH, 19). Stubborn it certainly is, for it persists as an agricultural weed in defiance of chemical spraying. 'Late germinating strains which miss the spray are probably being selected' is Terry Wells's explanation.

84

Geranium family, GERANIACEAE

CRANE'S-BILLS, *Geranium* spp.

Rather surprisingly, Clare has only one verse allusion, and that in a late lyric 'Early Morning' (LP, 481), to the 'beautiful blue' of our native Meadow Crane's-bill, *G. pratense*, which he had long before recommended to the author of *Flora Domestica* as 'a showy flower and a deal prettier than many of the geranium tribe raisd in pots' (NH, 22). In June 1825 he sent three other kinds of *Geranium* to a gardener friend – the Dusky Crane's-bill, *G. phaeum* (Clare calls it 'black'); the Pencilled Crane's-bill, *G. versicolor*; and a lilac-flowered one that may have been *G. phaeum* var. *lividum* (NH, 245). Though these are introduced and cultivated species, they often escape from gardens, so it is possible that Clare found them in the countryside.

Purple-loosestrife family, LYTHRACEAE

PURPLE-LOOSESTRIFE, *Lythrum salicaria* (plate 9)

Clare knew that the common name of this handsome waterside plant was Purple-loosestrife (NH, 22), but in his poetry he refers to it as 'long purple(s)', believing it to be the plant that Shakespeare calls by this name in his account of Ophelia's drowning. So when, in 'The Cross Roads', we learn that the forsaken Jane is in the habit of wading into water to pick 'gay long purple with its tufty spike' (EP II, 623), we can foresee how the story will end. In point of fact, Shakespeare meant Early-purple Orchids – Clare's 'cuckoos' – by the name, but at some time in the seventeenth or eighteenth century 'long purples' became associated with Purple-loosestrife – an association confirmed for generations of Shakespeare's readers by Millais's painting of the dead Ophelia.

Willowherb family, ONAGRACEAE

GREAT WILLOWHERB, *Epilobium hirsutum* (plate 10)

The country name of this colourful plant is still 'codlings and cream' or, in the East Midlands, 'coddled apples'. The 'idle boy' of one sonnet (Clare himself when young) 'crops the coddled apples for the smell' when pottering about in hot weather ('The ground is hard…', MP V, 373). Grigson insisted that neither leaves nor flowers have any smell and instead traced the name to Gerard's 'Codded [i.e. podded] Willow herbe'; but my own experience of crushing the leaves hard on a very hot day has convinced me that Clare had the better nose. Most British readers can repeat the experiment, for south of the Highlands one is never very far from a patch of Great Willowherb, although today Rosebay Willowherb, *Chamerion angustifolium*, thrusts itself more often on our notice.

COMMON EVENING-PRIMROSE, *Oenothera biennis*

Although it was already a known casual in the countryside, Clare's graceful lyric, 'Evening Primrose', was in all probability inspired by the sight of this American flower, which is pollinated by night-flying moths, growing in his own or a neighbour's garden:

> When once the sun sinks in the west
> And dew drops pearl the evenings breast
> All most as pale as moon beams are
> Or its companiable star
> The evening primrose opes anew
> Its delicate blossoms to the dew
> And shunning-hermit of the light
> Wastes its fair bloom upon the night
> Who blind fold to its fond caresses
> Knows not the beauty it posseses
> Thus it blooms on till night is bye

And day looks out with open eye
Bashed at the gaze it cannot shun
It faints and withers and is done   (MP IV, 260).

FUCHSIA, *Fuchsia* sp.

The oddest of all Clare's allusions to flowers must be this one from the pastiche of Byron's *Don Juan* that he wrote at High Beach; it is also apt and funny:

Don Juan was Ambassador from Russia
But had no hand in any sort of tax
His orders hung like blossoms of the fushia
And made the ladies hearts to melt like wax   (LP, 98).

ENCHANTER'S-NIGHTSHADE, *Circaea lutetiana*

'Walks in the Woods' (MP III, 572) ends with the poet taking home a bunch of woodland flowers that includes 'some few sprigs' of Enchanter's-nightshade. Both parts of the English name are misleading. 'Enchanter's' should be 'enchantress's', since, as the Latin name shows, it was once held by French herbalists ('*lutetiana*' means 'of Paris') to have been the plant used by Circe to transform members of Ulysses's crew into pigs. Nor has this rather drab weed of shady corners any resemblance to the nightshades. But Clare would have relished the Keatsian ring of the name as much as he would have delighted in the two-fold symmetry of the minute red and white flowers.

Sumach family, ANACARDIACEAE

STAG'S-HORN SUMACH, *Rhus typhina*

This brilliant shrub was one of the earliest introductions from North America. Clare as a young man would have read of it in Parkinson's *Paradisus* (1629) and could have admired it in the landscaping of Burghley

House (it was a Capability Brown favourite), but his only reference to it is in a late poem and is suggestive of such a well-planted Victorian shrubbery as Northampton's asylum may have possessed:

Here's the shumac all on fire
    Like hot coals amid the green
        ('Stanzas', ['The passing of a dream...'], LP 420).

Maple family, SAPINDACEAE

HORSE-CHESTNUT, *Aesculus hippocastanum*

When Clare was growing up the Horse-chestnut, introduced to Britain in the sixteenth century, was still limited for the most part to great estates: in the very early 'Narrative Verses, Written after An Excursion, from Helpston, to Burghley Park' he speaks admiringly of the park's 'towering chasenuts' (EP II, 7). But the tree that, on a day spent mostly in his garden in October 1824, he noticed was losing 'large hand shapd leaves that litter in yellow heaps round the trunk' (NH, 193) could have been one of the first Horse-chestnuts planted in a village setting for shade and visual effect – or even one grown from a conker by Clare himself.

SYCAMORE and FIELD MAPLE, *Acer* spp.

The dense foliage of the Sycamore, *A. pseudoplanatus*, meant in Clare's day different things to different classes. Avenues of the tree had been planted by aristocratic families such as the owners of Burghley Park at a time when the species was still, in Gerard's words, 'a stranger to England', and so not yet reviled for the stickiness of its fallen leaves that, John Evelyn was to complain, 'contaminate and mar our walks'. (The day when they would contaminate and mar our railtracks was even farther off.) Characteristically, Clare rejoices in the multitude of creatures attracted by this 'honeydew', which is a glutinous product of aphids:

Hark how the insects hum around and sing

Like happy ariels hid from heedless view
And merry bees that feed with eager wing
On the broad leaves glazed oer with honey dew
('The Sycamore', MP IV, 188).

By the late eighteenth century Sycamores, although no longer in favour with the rich for landscaping, were widely planted for shade and shelter by working farmers. In the June section of *The Shepherd's Calendar* the 'clipping pen' is situated under an elm or Sycamore, either of which would keep the unshorn sheep cool and the shorn ones dry (MP I, 78–9). Ultimately seeds from these homestead Sycamores would drift into woodland and produce the invasive monsters that we grumble at today for shutting out the light and impoverishing the ground flora. But by the side of a field, the shifting shadow of a 'splendid sycamore' would allow even buttercups to grow – as Clare's sonnet goes on to remind us.

The native Field Maple, *A. campestre*, with its more open habit of growth and its smaller, delicately pointed leaves, is little use as shelter. '[L]et us leave this maple tree', says one of Clare's shepherds, 'Or we shall soon be dripping wet' ('Lubin and Collin', EP I, 459). But everything else is in its favour as a woodland tree and the poet celebrates its virtues both in a swinging, colloquial song lyric, 'The Bonny Maple Tree', and in a sonnet, 'The Maple Tree'. The two poems enumerate its 'squatty, mossy stub' and bole ribbed like corduroy, its yellow-green young foliage, green tasselled flowers, fruit shaped like dragonfly wings or stag's horns, and dehiscent yellow leaves spotted with black. The song lyric ends with the maple as the home of nesting birds –

May the school boy, miss and spare em
And the speckled thrushes, rear em,
In the nest, above the arum,
On the bonny maple tree   (LP, 922)

– while the sonnet closes on the variety of ground flora that makes up the 'sweet clothing' of its trunk (LP, 1025). The amazing thing about these evocations of a much-loved plant in fine and exact detail is that they were written many years after Clare had been declared insane.

Rue family, RUTACEAE

RUE, *Ruta graveolens*

Like Shakespeare's Ophelia, whose fate she shares, Jane of 'The Cross Roads' (EP II, 628) is associated with Rue, which she once grew in her well-tended garden. Too bitter for a pot-herb, it had many medicinal uses.

Mallow family, MALVACEAE

MALLOWS, *Malva* spp.

'A beautiful wild mallow' that, according to Clare's comments on Elizabeth Kent's *Hibiscus*, 'grows on our heaths with pink flowers and frilld [i.e. deeply cut] leaves' (NH, 20) can only be the Musk-mallow, *M. moschata*, but it is the much smaller, pale-flowered and whole-leaved Dwarf Mallow, *M. neglecta*, also 'smelling faint of musk', that is gathered by the Village Doctress (MP III, 337) for her potions. She collects too the 'horseshoe leaves' of the Common Mallow, *M. sylvestris* (plate 15), and this is the plant that turns up again and again in Clare's poetry. Tall and spreading – 'fanned all abroad' is Clare's phrase ('Song' ['At closing day…'], LP, 553) – and bearing bright pink-purple flowers with a darker stripe, it grows almost anywhere but seems especially to favour the cleared area round a doorway: in a very late poem Clare remembers or imagines a house where

Horse shoe leav'd mallows wi plush satin flowers
All covered wi blossoms blush'd up to the doors
('Come in the morning', LP, 1011).

When the weary thresher of *The Shepherd's Calendar* looks back to the pleasures of his childhood, he remembers sitting on the doorstep and picking out of faded mallow flowers 'Each crumpld seed he calls a cheese' ('May', MP I, 69) – as Clare himself recalls doing in 'Childhood', where he says he and his friends hardly ever gave a mallow a chance to 'shake its seeds' (MP III, 237). We also learn from 'January: a Cottage Evening' that the flattish round nutlets served as beads to be threaded on long grass and were known to furnish the wheels for fairy chariots (MP I, 19).

Happily all these three species of *Malva* survive in the Soke today.

MARSH-MALLOW, A*lthaea officinalis*

'The marsh mallow grows in our fens', Clare writes in his notes on *Flora Domestica* (NH, 20). Despite all the drainage of the previous century, some of the fenland soil must have remained saline enough to support this estuarine plant, which is spectacularly beautiful in itself and was once of culinary as well as medical importance.

HOLLYHOCK, *Alcea rosea*

Since it has been escaping from gardens for centuries, this is likely to have been one of the five mallows that Clare claimed grew 'wild about us' (NH, 20) but his other allusions are all to it as a garden plant. An entry in his journal – 'the tall gaudy holliock with its mellancholy blooms stands bending to the wind and bidding the summer farwell' (NH, 175) – anticipates Tennyson in finding a pleasing melancholy in the flowers' late appearance. So do these lines, possibly intended for 'November' in *The Shepherd's Calendar*:

> When every flower forsakes the garden walks
> And not is left but brown and witherd stalks   *naught*
> The lingering holioak is latest seen
> Wi flowers and leaves half witherd and half green
> Bending wi oddling blooms on branches tall
> From wind and wet agen each cottage wall
> Lingering wi sumers memories many a day
> Till frosts chill fingers nips their bloom away

(MP I, 154; cf. 'Fragment' ['Tall holliocks in gaudy hues'], MP II, 270).

LIMES, *Tilia* spp.

In prehistoric times the Small-leaved Lime, *T. cordata*, was the pre-eminent tree of lowland England, and although it eventually yielded its dominance to other species, it grew in the Helpston area in Clare's day, as it continues to do in woods near the village. This is the lime that he names in 'Walks in the Woods' (MP III, 571) as part of the woodland understorey, along with Dogwood, Hawthorn, Spindle, Hazel and Crab Apple.

Today, however, the tree most of us know as Lime is *T.* × *europaea*, a cross between the native small-leaved and large-leaved species. Following the fashion set at Versailles and Hampton Court, landowners of the seventeenth and eighteenth centuries planted grand avenues of this hybrid. Burghley Park's famous mile-long double avenue of hundred-year-old limes had to be felled and replanted at the end of the last century; but in time it will look just as it did to Clare, whose long poem called 'The Progress of Rhyme', which is by way of being his *Biographia Literaria*, emphasises two of its features: the deep shade cast by 'Grain [i.e. bough] intertwisting into grain … Like ancient halls and minster aisles', and the 'everlasting hum' of bees busy among the powerfully scented flowers:

> As though twas natures very place
> Of worship where her mighty race
> Of insect life and spirits too
> In summer time were wont to go
> Both insects and the breath of flowers
> To sing their makers mighty powers
> Ive thought so as I used to rove
> Through burghley park that darksome grove
> Of Limes where twilight lingered grey
> Like evening in the midst of day …   (MP III, 498).

Small wonder that when the memory of this 'waked with time' (or, in Wordsworth's phrase, was recollected in tranquillity) it left Clare 'itching after ryhme'.

Mezereon family, THYMELAEACEAE

SPURGE-LAUREL, *Daphne laureola* (plate 16)

'Resolutely green' through the winter ('The Spindle Tree', MP IV, 330), this shrub also has flowers that 'shed a most beautiful perfume in the young spring mornings' (NH, 18). Clare records exactly where and when he once found it. On 21 November 1824 he explored the ruins of a manor house in the wood called Ashton Lawn and noted that the remaining walls were surrounded by Blackthorn, Privet and Spurge-laurel (NH, 206). When, some years later, the site was plundered for stone with which to build a road, he wrote to the wood's owner to protest (*Letters*, 553) – with what success we do not know, but the ruins can still be seen there, and so, nearly two centuries on, can the Spurge-laurel.

Rock-rose family, CISTACEAE

COMMON ROCK-ROSE, *Helianthemum nummularium* (plate 14)

William Pitt (not the politician), who made a survey of Northamptonshire agriculture when Clare was a child, commented on 'little sun-flowers… occupying the whole surface of the ground to a considerable extent in some situations between King's Cliffe and Wansford' – that is, on the calcareous grasslands to the west of Helpston. The agricultural reforms Pitt advocated have since restricted Common Rock-roses to a sprinkling of sites, but they remain a cherished feature of the area. Because they thrive in full sun, they show a liking for small eminences: hillocks left by stone-quarrying at Barnack Hills and Holes, and anthills in such pastures as remain. In Clare's long poem 'Birds Nesting', a whitethroat nests on the open heath close to an anthill 'thickly topt / With wild rock roseys lemon blooms' (MP II, 168).

Plate 1: Some woodland flowers of the spring

Bluebells and Early-purple Orchid, Clare's 'Bluebells and cuckoo's in the
    wood' (pp. 176, 169 and 171)

Lords-and-Ladies, whose 'spindle flowers their cases burst' (pp. 159–160)

Bluebells, at first known to Clare as 'harebells' (p. 176)

Plate 2: More woodland flowers of the spring
Herb-Paris, found by Clare 'in Oxey Wood' (p. 163)
Common Twayblade, found by Clare in a number of local woods (p. 166)
Lesser Celandine, 'like a bright star spring-tempted from the sky', and
    Primrose, 'with its little brunny eye' (pp. 38 and 107)

Plate 3: Further flowers of the spring
Lesser Celandine, Clare's 'crow flower', 'buttercup' or 'pilewort', unrelated to
  Greater Celandine (p. 38)
Fly Orchid, found by Clare 'in Oxey Wood', but no longer there (p. 171)
Cowslips, 'increasing like crowds at a fair' (p. 108)

Plate 4: Spring trees and shrubs

Pedunculate Oak, with male catkins that Clare called 'little green shaggy trails' (p. 69)

European Larch, a deciduous conifer about which Clare wrote 'There's no flowers more red, than the flowers of the larch' (p. 26)

Blackthorn, with its 'snowy blossoms' on 'naked hedges' (p. 53)

Plate 5: Rare flowers of grassland
Green-winged Orchid, Clare's 'pasture cuckoo's', now surviving mainly in
  nature reserves (p. 171)
Burnt Orchid, Clare's 'Red Man', no longer found locally (p. 170)
Pasqueflower, which Clare almost fancied 'sprang from the blood or dust of
  the romans' (p. 36)

Plate 6: More grassland plants

Adder's-tongue, an unusual fern of meadows (p. 21)

Bee Orchid, a species still found near where Clare knew it (p. 172)

Common Eyebright, with 'slightly penciled flowers', gathered 'for weak short sighted eyes' (p. 133)

Plate 7: Hedgerow shrubs and climbers

Dog-rose, as it 'swells its prickly buds anew' (pp. 61–2)

Old-man's-beard, the fruits of Traveller's-joy, called 'goat's beard' by Clare (pp. 36–7)

Hawthorn, its stamens being Clare's 'pinky heads like fairy pins' (p. 56)

Plate 8: Some flowers of wet places
Yellow Iris, 'fine enough to be garden flowers' (p. 173)
Yellow Loosestrife, which likes 'splashy places' (p. 111)
Meadowsweet, which 'taunts [tosses] high its showy wreath' (p. 57)

Plate 9: More flowers of wet places
Purple-loosestrife, believed by Clare to be Shakespeare's 'long purples' (p. 84)
Ragged-Robin, with 'much finer flowers than pinks' (p. 103)
Marsh-marigold, 'horse blob' or 'mare blob' in Northamptonshire (p. 33)

Plate 10: Further flowers of wet places

Great Willowherb or 'coddled apples', which Clare as an 'idle boy' cropped
'for the smell' (p. 85)

Water Dock, which 'on the bank reddens high' (p. 101)

Flowering-rush, used by a boy in one of Clare's poems to decorate his hat
(p. 161)

Plate 11: Some heathland flowers
Harebells, for Clare 'little bell flowers', 'heath bells' or 'harvest bells'
    (pp. 136–7)
Betony, described by Clare as 'medicinal' (p. 127)
Gorse, on 'heaths oerspread with furze blooms sunny shine' (p. 51)

Plate 12: Some flowers of Barnack Hills and Holes
Clustered Bellflower, recorded by Clare from 'hilly ground' (p. 136)
Dark Mullein, with flowers 'of a bright yellow with purple threads in the middle' (p. 126)
Ploughman's-spikenard, the 'spicey smell' of which interested Clare (p. 142)

Plate 13: More flowers of Barnack Hills and Holes

Man Orchid, Clare's 'Green Man' (pp. 169–170)

Autumn Gentian or Felwort, a late flower of limestone grassland
   (pp. 114–115)

Greater Knapweed, 'knob weeds blood red on the hill' (p. 140)

Plate 14: Summer flowers

Common Poppies and Cornflowers, the latter nowadays mainly sprung from
sown wild-flower seed (pp. 30 and 140–1)

Scarlet Pimpernel, 'with its eye of gold and scarlet starry points of flowers'
(p. 111)

Common Rock-rose and Wild Thyme on an anthill (pp. 92 and 130–1)

Plate 15: Some examples of folklore
Common Poppy capsule with its 'straw bonnet' (p. 30)
Greater Celandine or 'wart weed' because its yellow latex was believed to
    remove warts (p. 31)
Common Mallow, a flower and a 'cheese' (p. 89)

Plate 16: Wintertime
Spurge-laurel, 'resolutely green' through the winter (p. 92)
Lichen on a tree trunk, as if it was 'whitewashed every year' (p. 17)
Winter Aconites, with 'green leaf frilling round their cups of gold' (p. 34)

Mignonette family, RESEDACEAE

MIGNONETTES, *Reseda* spp.

Watching honey bees forage in his garden, Clare discovered that on each journey they kept to a single kind of flower: 'another began with the miginette and gathered honey from that only' (NH, 270). This would have been the Garden Mignonette, *R. odorata*. It may have been the memory of its strongly scented flowers that caused Clare, at High Beach and very homesick, to write that in Epping Forest mugwort bloomed 'like mignonette' ('To the Nightingale', LP, 16), although he could equally well have been remembering the less fragrant Wild Mignonette, *R. lutea*, still to be found in the Soke today.

A third member of this genus, Weld, *R. luteola*, appears in 'Cowper Green' as 'wild wad' (EP II, 183). This has misled commentators into thinking Clare is writing about the blue-dye plant, Woad, *Isatis tinctoria*. But the 'tall wild Woad that lifts its spirey tops / By stone pits' in 'Valentine Eve' (MP III, 77) cannot be *Isatis*, a plant with loosely bushy flower-heads, and in fact can only be Weld – also a dye plant – that still lifts its tapering and slightly spiralling inflorescences in Swaddywell Pit and other stony places near Helpston.

Cabbage family, BRASSICACEAE

Easily recognised by the criss-cross arrangement of their petals in fours (hence the old name of Cruciferae), the plants of this family, though their flowers are seldom of any great beauty unless they are cultivated, tend to be of agricultural importance either as vegetables and herbs or as the weeds that compete with them. So it is not surprising to find so many of them in Clare's poems of rural life.

WALLFLOWER, *Erysimum cheiri*

The Northamptonshire name of 'blood walls' is a good one, for the flowers are often a deep rusty red and the plant itself, a garden favourite for its colour and 'lucious smell' ('June', MP I, 81), has long been naturalised on old masonry; in 'Pleasures of Spring' Clare finds 'Blood walls glowing with rich tawney streaks' on a ruined tower (MP III, 65). Another popular name of the time, 'gillyflower', occurs in his sad lines on the celibacy of asylum existence:

> The Gilafers a Gilafer
> And nature owns the plan
> And strange a thing it is to me
> A man cant be a man   ('To Miss B.', LP, 514)

That 'Gilafer' here means Wallflower is confirmed by Anne Baker, who quotes these lines, still at the time unpublished, in her 1854 glossary of Northamptonshire words. But according to the passage in 'June', 'white and purple jiliflowers' grow alongside 'bloodwalls', indicating that Clare had, at an earlier time, used this name for a different flower. See the entry under 'Brompton Stock' on p. 99.

SHEPHERD'S-PURSE, *Capsella bursa-pastoris*

Children easily recognise this small weed by its heart-shaped seed-pods, though very few of them will ever have met a shepherd, let alone one with a drawstring pouch at his belt such as gave the plant its name in medieval times. There is something very satisfying in the fact that this plant with its centuries-old name helped to restore Clare's sense of place just after the move to Northborough had left him badly disorientated:

> this 'shepherds purse' that grows
> In this strange spot – In days gone bye
> Grew in the little garden rows
> Of my old home now left – And I

Feel what I never felt before
This weed an ancient neighbour near...
      ('The Flitting', MP III, 488).

Eighteen springs on, and much further away from his old home, it was still giving him a pleasure that slips into the song, 'I' the sunshine o' the Season...', about 'lovely Dinah', who is encountered in a road where 'The Shepherds purse and groundsell too were breaking into bloom' ('Song', LP, 265).

WINTER-CRESS, *Barbarea vulgaris*

The poem on 'Spring' quoted from in the entry on 'Garlic Mustard' (see p. 98 below) also contains an allusion to 'the yellow rocket by the dyke side' (LP, 987). In the sombre winter landscape of the Fens, the deep green foliage that gives this very common plant its more familiar name of Winter-cress would have been as pleasing to Clare as were its dense yellow flower-heads in April.

WATER-CRESS, *Nasturtium officinale*

'The Widow or Cress Gatherer' tells the story of an impoverished woman who struggles to make a living by

> Dragging the sprouting cresses from the brooks
> A savory sallad sought for luxurys whim   (EP II, 653).

That Water-cress was still thought of as a delicacy suggests that the popular demand for it, which became intense once its anti-scorbutic properties were known, had not yet reached the Midlands in 1820.

CUCKOOFLOWER, *Cardamine pratensis*

Clare would have been dismayed to discover that the accepted name of this delicately coloured crucifer of damp meadows is now

'Cuckooflower', since this was the name, usually shortened to 'cuckoo', that he jealously guarded for his beloved Early-purple Orchids. In a note on *Cardamine* in Elizabeth Kent's *Flora Domestica* he writes 'this is calld lilac with us as well as "ladysmock" but I never heard it calld cuckoo in my life otherwise then by books' (NH, 15). He uses 'lilac' in his first published volume and 'ladysmock' thereafter, although in 'Wood Rides' (MP IV, 349) he notes that his fellow-villagers used the latter name for Wood Anemones: 'lady smocks so called by toil'.

COMMON WHITLOWGRASS, *Erophila verna*

One of Clare's sonnets describes his walk to work on a spring morning, when

> Flowers thicken every where the very tops
> Of walls are thronged with springs delicious crops
> Of tiney snow white blossoms thickly spread
> > ('How beautiful is daybreak', MP IV, 387).

The small and perky Common Whitlowgrass, which can root in the smallest crack in a limestone wall, strikes me as the best of the suggestions that have been made for this plant's identity; it is also the most authoritative, as it was made by the late Richard Fitter.

CABBAGES and TURNIP, *Brassica* spp.

Ordinary Cabbages, *B. oleracea*, along with unspecified 'greens', are grown by the thrifty cottagers Dobson and Judie (EP I, 179); and Broccoli, *B. oleracea* var. *botrytis* 'Asparagoides', appears in a late fragment of verse (LP, 901). But the only member of this genus that really makes its presence felt in Clare's poetry is the humble Turnip, *B. rapa*. He knew it intimately from having worked several seasons alongside of 'old John Cue ... at turnip hoeing for which he was famous' (NH, 220); knew, for example, that even if the plants were kept free from weeds, they could be devoured by pests:

> soon as ere the turnip creeps
> From out the crust burnt soil and peeps
> Upon the farmers watching eye
> Tis eaten by the jumping flye   (MP I, 96).

Clare's publisher John Taylor rejected these lines, along with the whole first version of 'July': 'I cannot make a Volume fit to be seen out of such Materials' (*Letters*, 358). But the flea beetle was no trivial matter in Helpston, for the survival of stock in winter depended on a good supply of turnips. Several passages in Clare's verse describe sheep in snowy fields where, however they may 'loath their frozen food' ('Winter' ['The morning wakens…'], EP II, 584), they

> gnaw the frozen turnip to the ground
> With sharp quick bite and then go noising round
> The boy that pecks the turnips all the day
> And knocks his hands to keep the cold away
>   ('The sheep get up…', MP V, 252).

But even the shepherd boy is less wretched than the mole catcher or tramp whom hunger drives to 'Stoop down a turnip from the sheep to steal', and eat it raw: a sharp reminder, in this present flowery context, that life in Clare's countryside was not all roses ('The Mole Catcher', MP II, 27; cf. 'He eats a moments stoppage…', MP V, 270).

CHARLOCK, *Sinapis arvensis*

Pointing out to his children a turnip field 'littered with gold', Clare calls Charlock 'a troublesome weed'. But in the very next line of 'A Holiday Walk' (MP III, 403) it is 'a beautiful sight in the distance', and the poet repeatedly registered his delight at the brilliant yellow that Charlock added to the red and blue of poppies and Cornflowers in a wheat field or to the copper hue of a clover field (*By Himself*, 38; cf. the fragment at MP II, 162): sights now lost to us, though Charlock has proved more resistant than most other weeds to modern herbicides.

HEDGE MUSTARD, *Sisymbrium officinale*

Clare's gipsy friends had their own names for many wild plants, among them 'burvine' for 'a little plant with a hard stem that grows in villages and waste places one sort bearing yellow flowers and another purple ones' (*By Himself*, 85). Plainly the name is a corruption of 'vervain', but that plant, *Verbena officinalis* (see p. 135), has only purple flowers. For an explanation of the yellow ones we must go to F. H. Perring's additions to Druce's list of Clare's plants: 'in the days of the herbalists the hedge mustard and the vervain were both included in the genus *Verbena* (or *Verbenaca*), being distinguished … as *V. foemina* and *V. mas* (or *mascula*)'.

Hedge Mustard's hard stem, commented on in a thirteenth-century herbal, has earned it the modern name of 'the barbed-wire weed'. In the nineteenth century it was sometimes known as 'flixweed', although incorrectly so since this derivative from 'flux weed' is the English name for another crucifer, *Descurainia sophia*. Clare seems to have picked up the name by 1832, when he wrote 'Langley Bush' (MP V, 5–6), a poem recalling the countryside round that landmark as it had been in his boyhood. Nearby Castor Hanglands, also alluded to in the poem, was the setting for an encampment of Clare's gipsy friends, and his recollection of their plant lore could have brought with it the memory of 'The tiney flix weeds only flower': Hedge Mustard's minute yellow blossom at the end of each whippy stem.

GARLIC MUSTARD or JACK-BY-THE-HEDGE, *Alliaria petiolata*

In the best of several poems called 'Spring' that Clare wrote in the Northampton asylum, 'Hedge weeds all juicy run up tall' and among them,

Above the Quick set hedge blooms 'Jack by the hedge'
His white flowers shine all down the narrow lane
In April sunshine still a welcome pledge
To show warm weather brings wild flowers again
('In every step we tread…', LP, 987)

– sunlit pleasure recalled also by Geoffrey Grigson: 'In a brilliant sunshine, in May, one is always freshly struck by platoons of this familiar plant, at starched attention, the starch-white flowers above the new green leaves and against the green bank.'

BROMPTON STOCK, *Matthiola incana*

Among the cottage garden flowers in the June section of *The Shepherd's Calendar* are 'white and purple jiliflowers that stay / Lingering in blossom summer half away' (MP I, 81). Gillyflowers cannot here be Wallflowers, since those are named in the next couplet as 'blood walls'. Dame's-violet, *Hesperis matronalis*, is a possible identification. But the garden crucifer with the longest flowering time is Brompton Stock, a cultivated form developed in a famous London nursery from the fragrant wild Hoary Stock, *M. incana*. Clare grew it in the mid 1820s from seed given him by friends (NH, 246, 247), and many years later he could think of no higher compliment to a pretty girl than to say she was sweeter than 'Brompton stocks perfume at eve' ('Oh Susan my dearest', LP, 1063).

Bastard-toadflax family, SANTALACEAE

The former Mistletoe family, Viscaceae, is now absorbed into this family.

MISTLETOE, *Viscum album*

In an early attempt at 'fine writing', 'The Woodman or the Beauties of a Winter Forest', Clare tells us that his forester's 'simple soul is warmly and venerably inspired when he views the beautiful clumps of mizzletoe growing on the leafless branches of the aged thorn' (NH, 5) and goes on to make him speculate – improbably – about its worship by Druids. We have to wait till the December section of *The Shepherd's Calendar* for a more natural response to Mistletoe:

The shepherd now no more afraid
Since custom doth the chance bestow

Starts up to kiss the giggling maid
Beneath the branch of mizzletoe
That neath each cottage beam is seen
Wi pear[l]-like-berrys shining gay ...   (MP I, 158).

One wonders if the fact that every cottage once had its Christmas bunch has contributed to Mistletoe now being only occasionally met with in the district – outside, that is, of gardens and parkland such as that of Burghley House, where 'it hangs on from virtually every lime tree in the approach avenue' (GW2, 221). But the destruction of hedgerows is a more likely reason for its decline, since its commonest host in the countryside is Hawthorn.

Thrift family, PLUMBAGINACEAE

THRIFT, *Armeria maritima*

Clare's 'Summer Ballad' (MP IV, 140–2) is an idealised portrait of a country girl such as the reader may imagine his twin sister would have been, had she lived. Thrift – a coastal wild flower, but a garden flower inland – is among the plants that delight her in a neighbour's flowerbeds.

Knotweed family, POLYGONACEAE

DOCKS and SORRELS, *Rumex* spp.

Like the tired and thirsty mower in 'July' (MP I, 89), Clare would often have sucked the leaves of the Common Sorrel, *R. acetosa*, which he knew as 'sour grass'. Their sharp taste may have brought back bittersweet memories of his friendship with Richard Turnill, who had died young, and so have led to the writing of a sonnet that recalls the fish they caught together, the 'few old books' they bought, and how, as they roamed the fields, they 'often stooped for hunger on the way / And eat the sour grass in the meadow hay' ('Turnill, we toiled ...', MP V, 249).

The village boys who, in the sonnet beginning 'I love to wander by the ivy bank' (MP V, 377), 'pulled the docks and called them milking cows' (because of the teat-like roots?) would not have distinguished between the Curled Dock, R. *crispus*, and the Broad-leaved Dock, R. *obtusifolius*, and nor did Clare in his descriptions of neglected gardens and farmyards. His only use of the expression 'broad leafd dock' is in a context that makes clear he means an altogether different plant, the Greater Burdock (see p. 138).

In contrast with these two generally despised species, Water Dock, R. *hydrolapathum* (plate 10), was much loved by nineteenth-century landscape painters. Its height and colour catch the eye of the Clare family on their 'Walk in the Fields': 'a tall water dock on the bank reddens high' (MP III, 378).

Pink family, CARYOPHYLLACEAE

STITCHWORTS and CHICKWEEDS, *Stellaria* spp.

It is the tenth of February and warm for the time of year, but the birds are not singing ('Birds: Why are ye silent?', LP 959–60). We can only assume that the goldfinches picking seeds out of the 'bunches o chickweed / Wi' small starry flow'rs' are too busy replacing their energy to sing. Fortunately for them, the tough and prolific Common Chickweed, *S. media*, flowers and seeds all the year round.

An early poem, 'Address to an Insignificant Flower...', tells us more about Clare's regret for his own obscurity than it does about the plant (EP I, 216). But the description he gave when he alluded to the poem a few years later – 'a little white starry flower with pale green grassy leaves grows by woodsides and among bushes' (NH, 23) – leaves us in no doubt that it was Greater Stitchwort, *S. holostea*. He must have been told the name at some later date, since 'stitchwort' crops up casually in one of his last poems ('An Anecdote of Love', LP, 1013).

MOUSE-EARS, *Cerastium* spp.

Some twenty years after the early poem referred to in the last entry – years in which he acquired fame and subsequently lost it – Clare wrote a poem about another plant for which he had no name. This time, however, he says enough about the white, starry, 'chickweed zembling flowers' for us to hazard a guess that he means the Common Mouse-ear, *C. fontanum*. Fellow-feeling ('I often felt my lowly lot / As couzin unto thine') leads him to rescue the plant from trampling feet and burrowing moles, and brings the poem to a graceful ending, indicative of how far he has come both as poet and person:

Then may thy little lot attend
On me till life shall close
To meet the notice of a friend
And be unknown to foes
    ('Thou little tiney namless thing…', MP V, 127).

After the description of the Greater Stitchwort quoted in the preceding entry, Clare adds that 'there is one in gardens much like it the flower is exactly the same but the leaves is a whooly [i.e. woolly] or silvery green' (NH, 23). This is a good description of the Snow-in-summer, *C. tomentosum*, of cottage garden borders.

CORNCOCKLE, *Agrostemma githago*

Though it is described in 'A Walk in the Fields' (MP III, 381) as 'less showy' than poppies, the Corncockle's star formation of long spiky sepals and streaked magenta petals make it a strikingly beautiful flower. In 'There's something in the time' (LP, 885), 'the cockle's streaky eyes' act as a marker for locating a lark's nest in a cornfield. This suggests that it did not grow with the same profusion as the poppies and Cornflowers that open the poem; and Terry Wells doubts that it ever was such a locally common weed of agriculture in the Soke of Peterborough as Druce maintained that it was in his day. What *is* certain is that in the second half of last century effective methods of seed-cleansing rendered the Corncockle extinct as a wild flower. Today, in order to gain some notion of what a small area of wheatfield gay with poppies, Cornflowers, Corncockles and Corn Marigolds looked like in Clare's time, one has to pay a July visit to a nature reserve where these agricultural weeds are specially grown, such as College Lake, Tring.

CAMPIONS, *Silene* spp.

In the molecular system of classification, the former Catchfly genus, Lychnis, and the former Campion genus, Silene, have been brought together under the latter name.

In his note on Elizabeth Kent's rather perfunctory entry for the many garden species of 'Catchfly' in her *Flora Domestica*, Clare writes: 'my "ragged robin" is I believe a species of it and a much more beautiful flower in my opinion mine grows wild by the side of brooks and rivers with a narrow leaf just like a catchflye and a cluster of flowers on the top of several stalks from the same root of a beautiful bright pink colour jagged about the edges as if they had been torn' (NH, 17). This enthusiasm for Ragged-Robin, *S. flos-cuculi* (plate 9), is shared by the hero of 'Valentine Eve':

> The ragged robbin by the runnel brinks
> Seemed in his eye much finer flowers than pinks   (MP III, 77).

Ragged-Robins, or 'meadow pinks' as Clare learnt to call them at Northampton, spring up at several places in his poetry, and always near water. Yet this is not a streamside plant, though it needs to be damp. The association with water conceivably goes back to the experience of being sent by his haymaking father on a very hot day to get water from Round Oak Spring and noticing how parched the flowers, especially the Ragged-Robins, looked beside the stream flowing from the wellhead. This etched itself into his memory for two reasons: one, that it inspired him to write one of his best poems, 'Noon' ('All how silent and how still', EP I, 404; see *By Himself*, p. 110); the other that, soon afterwards, the scene in which the episode was set changed completely as a result of the Enclosures. All the vegetation along the watercourse was removed, leaving spring and stream 'naked', as Clare was to lament in poem after poem – most passionately in 'The Lamentations of Round-Oak Waters' (EP I, 228) and most movingly almost twenty years later in 'Round Oak Spring' (MP IV, 280).

In Elizabeth Kent's alphabetically arranged book there is no other mention of plants of this genus until we get to 'Lychnis', when she writes at length on 'the Common Meadow Lychnis ... generally known by the name of Rose Campion'. At this point in his reading Clare declares himself glad to come upon his Ragged-Robin at last, and in fact 'Ragged-robin' is one of many local names cited by Kent. But it is clear from her description that the species she is writing about is the Red Campion, *S. dioica*. Clare failed to realise this, for the good reason that he had never set eyes upon this very common and widespread – and beautiful – flower, which was absent from a large area to the south of the Wash; Charles Darwin, a student at Christ's College at the time Clare was writing his best poetry, remarked on its absence from Cambridgeshire. It is still rare in the Soke and has only recently appeared in the environs of Helpston – possibly with the help of a wild-flower seed packet or two.

The Red Campion has, however, a close relation in the White Campion, *S. latifolia*, with which it freely hybridises, so when he read that Kent's Rose Campion is 'of a bright rose-colour; sometimes white' Clare noted that 'we have the white with us wild and often in gardens'. On 27 November 1824 Clare's own garden acquired a 'tall white Lychnis' (NH, 207) as a present from Henderson, and on the strength of this journal entry Clare has been credited with the first county record for White Campion. But as Grainger points out, Henderson is unlikely to have sent Clare a plant so familiar to them both. In fact his covering letter names the plant he sent as 'Lychnidia', which suggests it was a white form of the Rose-of-Heaven – formally named *Lychnidia coeli-rosa* in 1870 but presumably already known by the name – now called *Silene coeli-rosa*. However, that is not a particularly tall garden *Silene*: a better candidate might be a white form of *S. coronaria*, generally known to gardeners as Rose Campion.

PINKS and CARNATIONS, *Dianthus* spp.

The Common Pink, *Dianthus plumarius*, is pale pink or white with narrow leaves, and the Clove Pink, *D. caryophyllus*, is a deeper pink with wider leaves and a stronger fragrance that makes it 'the sweetest flower that grows' for the narrator of 'The Sorrows of Love' (MP I, 168). Both were favourite cottage garden flowers in Clare's time. So were the Carnations that seventeenth-century 'florists' (i.e. plant breeders) had developed from Clove Pinks: the cottagers Dobson and Judie in the poem of that name grow them 'As well for pleasure as for use' (EP I, 179). But what use? Though they are called 'clipping pinks' in 'June' (MP I, 82), there cannot have been much sale for cut flowers in a village. Would the old couple have made from them the hangover cure described in Hill's *Family Herbal* as a 'pleasant syrup for disturbances of the head'?

Clare himself appears to have been an enthusiastic grower of pinks and carnations: he owned three published guides to these and other florists' flowers, and among his manuscripts is a copy of a list made to accompany cuttings, or young plants, of fourteen varieties of pink. It concludes with a mention of '8 sorts from Burghley which you may have *pipings* [i.e. cuttings] of next year' (NH, 351). 'You' is possibly Henderson, although Clare had other gardening friends with whom he exchanged plants.

Goosefoot family, AMARANTHACEAE

LOVE-LIES-BLEEDING, *Amaranthus caudatus*

An early import from America (Gerard grew it in his garden), this plant takes its name from the heavy red flower-heads which trail on the ground. Clare uses its name to full effect when he has the narrator of 'The Cross Roads' (EP II, 628) recall 'True love lies bleeding' as one of the plants in the garden that Jane grew up in: Jane drowns herself when she is abandoned by her lover.

Dogwood family, CORNACEAE

DOGWOOD, *Cornus sanguinea*

Clare never calls this widespread shrub 'dogwood'. For him, it is the 'Cornel' that forms part of the understorey in 'Walks in the Woods' (MP III, 571) or the 'Corn tree' that in January 1825 he notes is coming into early leaf in Simons Wood (NH, 220; another botanical first record).

But when he is writing of the brilliant first-year stems, 'red as stock doves claws' ('Pleasures of Spring', MP III, 53) which have earned it its American name of 'bloodtwig', he calls it 'foul rice' or 'foulroyce' – a name recorded in Joseph Wright's *English Dialect Dictionary*, but without any explanation, as the name given to Dogwood in the neighbouring county of Rutland.

Balsam family, BALSAMINACEAE

BALSAM, *Impatiens* sp.

A letter from Joseph Henderson dated 5 April 1830 shows that on that date he sent Clare the seeds of a balsam which could be depended upon to flower well – 'I brought it here with me in 1815 and I have had nothing so good for the last five or six years'. Orange Balsam, *I. capensis*, introduced from North America in the previous century, is a possibility. It could not have been the invasive though magnificent Indian (or Himalayan) Balsam, *I. glandulifera*, which was not introduced until a decade later.

Jacob's-ladder family, POLEMONIACEAE

PHLOX, *Phlox* sp.

This is a flower that we know was in Clare's garden, because Henderson sent his friend a 'White Phlox' on Christmas Day, 1824. The species could have been one of several eighteenth-century introductions from North America: the night-scented *P. paniculata* from the eastern seaboard is one possibility.

Primrose family, PRIMULACEAE

AURICULA, PRIMROSE and COWSLIP, *Primula* spp.

'I send you the Auricula which I promised, pray how do you proceed as a Florist'? Henderson asked Clare in May, 1822. 'Florist' at that time meant someone who developed, for exhibiting, pot-grown varieties from one or other of a small number of genera, including the Auricula, *P. auricula* –

> velvet 'raculas bepowderd flower
> That lookd as someone in an idle hour
> Had stooped adown to dust em oer wi meal
>
>   ('The Sorrows of Love', MP I, 169).

Clare could not afford to buy the mature Auricula plants of which he copied down the names and prices from catalogues. But helped by the books on floristry that he began to collect about this time, he was able to grow them himself from offsets given him by Henderson and perhaps other friends – successfully it would seem, because in the autumn of 1824 he set about making something he calls 'a shed for my Ariculas' (NH, 193). More usually termed a 'stage' or more recently a 'theatre', this was an open-sided structure with shelves on which the potted Auriculas were placed at flowering time. Dark boarding behind the shelves served to show off the mealy whiteness of the plants' leaves and the brilliant colours of their flowers. Further journal entries for 1825 – 'made a new frame for my Ariculas' on 26 May and 'Finished planting my Ariculas' on 3 June (NH, 242, 244) – suggest that once flowering was over Clare, as recommended, removed the plants to a frame.

Apart from a mention in 'Contentment' (LP, 588) of 'powdered flowers' that Clare or his transcriber absent-mindedly wrote down as 'Bears-breach' (instead of 'bear's-ears', the popular name for Auriculas), the lines quoted above are the only reference in Clare's verse to the highly-cultivated Auricula. In contrast there are two hundred or so to the native Primrose, *P. vulgaris* (plate 2), which bloomed almost the year round in Helpston woods and hedgerows, and a few of them are spot on:

> With its little brunny eye
> And its yellow rim so pale
> And its crimp and curdled leaf
> Who can pass its beautys by?
>
>   ('The Primrose Bank', MP III, 543).

Elsewhere, however, Clare's attempts to capture the flower's unique colour by the hard mineral terms 'sulphur' and 'brimstone' (or, worse, 'jaundice-tinctured') sound forced and so do descriptions of it in his late poetry as 'burning'. Dozens of other allusions are merely perfunctory.

Two explanations of this suggest themselves. One is that poets felt constrained in writing about the flower after Wordsworth condemned Peter Bell for seeing 'a primrose by a river's brim' as nothing more than a yellow primrose – until D. H. Lawrence sensibly asked, what more did he want it to be? Another is to be found in the reception of Clare's first collection, *Poems Descriptive of Rural Life and Scenery*. Reviewers picked out for special praise a sonnet, 'The Primrose', which Clare himself already considered one of his best efforts. As a result, the flower became his poetic signature – and signatures are something that, after our first proud flourishes, we come to write mechanically.

If Clare's Primroses often disappoint, it is quite otherwise with his Cowslips, *Primula veris* (plate 3). When, in his version of the 148th Psalm, he replaces the psalmist's 'fruitful trees' with English wild flowers, Cowslips are the first to be called upon to praise their Creator:

> Bowing adorers of the gale
> Ye cowslips delicatly pale
>   Upraise your loaded stems
> Unfold your cups in splendour speak
> Who deckt you in that ruddy streak
>   And gilt your golden gems
>
>   ('Song of Praise', EP II, 604).

These lines reflect the intense pleasure that this 'very favourite flower' (NH, 18) gives Clare year after year, from the time the first 'quaking cowslip fearfully un[kn]otts' in 'Spring' ('There is sweet feelings...', EP II, 462) to warm days in May when Cowslips, 'Increasing like crowds at a fair', turn the meadows 'from green to gold' ('The Cowslips', LP, 34; 'Mary a Ballad', LP, 512). And this annual transformation reassures him that the flower will be

As fresh two thousand years to come as now
With those five crimson spots upon its brow
        ('The Eternity of Nature', MP III, 528).

This year-by-year continuity serves also to link Clare's days each to each, so that he is able, in the Northampton asylum, to recall 'the cowslip close' where, thirty years earlier, he and Patty

    both looked on the self same thing
    Till both became as one
        ('Clare to his Wife', LP, 650).

    Cowslips were important in May Day customs when Clare was a child. The flowers lent themselves to being strung into garlands, or hung over a short length of thread which was then pulled tight to make a cowslip ball. In 'Sport in the Meadows', children pour into the fields for their May Day Cowslips, chasing off the cows as they do so:

As though there wa'n't a cows lap peep to spare
– For they want some for tea and some for wine
And some to maken up a cuck a ball
To throw across the garlands silken line
That reaches oer the street from wall to wall   (MP III, 451).

The cows here remind us that 'cowslip' means 'cow pat', which may explain why many Victorians preferred to call the flower by another long-established country name, 'paigle'; Clare picked this up at High Beach, but soon reverted to the more familiar 'cowslip'.
    For centuries before Clare's time, P. vulgaris and P. veris had been welcomed into gardens, especially if they were interesting natural sports such as the pink or white primroses that he found in the Helpston woods (NH, 21, 235). It was from such mutants that the Elizabethans had developed varieties of the kind he noted down from catalogues: 'Double Pink Primrose' (NH, 349) and 'Westons Hose in hose' (i.e. with one corolla inside another – NH, 350). The 'Red primroses', however, that occur in

the late 'A Valentine' (LP, 301) were a seventeenth-century introduction from Europe or the Levant.

Primroses and Cowslips hybridise freely (Linnaeus thought them a single species) and the resulting *P.* × *polyantha* (*P. vulgaris* × *P. veris*) is the 'oxlip' of Shakespeare and other poets. Clare – who presumably never saw the true Oxlip, *P. elatior*, which in Britain is an East Anglian speciality – makes no use of the word 'oxlip', and there is strong evidence that his name for the hybrid was 'Bedlam Cowslip' (or 'Bedlam Primrose'). A late poem speaks of this as a plant with 'twenty blossoms on a stalk', which suggests hybrid vigour ('The winter time is over...', LP, 169). Moreover, Anne Baker, who was able to consult Clare when compiling her *Glossary of Northamptonshire Words and Phrases*, defines the 'bedlam cowslip' as 'The Paigle, or larger kind of Cowslip', quoting a song then still in manuscript in which Clare writes of it growing 'safe neath the hazzle, of thicket and woods' ('I pluck summer blossoms...', LP, 270). But when Clare's Journal was published in 1951, botanists were puzzled by an entry under 17 February 1825: 'Saw a large bunch of blue violets in flower and a root of the Bedlam Cowslip' (NH, 224). How could Clare have recognised the False Oxlip just from its young foliage? So the plant was re-identified as Lungwort, *Pulmonaria officinalis*, known in Oxfordshire as the bedlam (i.e. Bethlehem) cowslip and called the cowslip of Jerusalem by Elizabeth Kent, which can be found naturalised in shady places and which could have been distinguished at an early stage by the white spots on its leaves. On the other hand, Clare can well have been struck by cowslip-shaped leaves, such as a hybrid might have, showing so early in the year. So here is a problem that must for the present remain unresolved.

Hybrids between Primroses and Cowslips also played a part in the creation of another florists' flower, the Garden Polyanthus, which came into existence in the middle of the seventeenth century, in all probability as the result of a cross between the False Oxlip and the introduced Red Primrose already referred to. One of Clare's last poems alludes to 'poly anthus peeps with blebs of dew' ('The spring is come...', LP, 1104): a recollection, perhaps, of flowers that his journal shows him to have grown in his Helpston garden – some of them from seed given him by Eliza Emmerson (NH, 245, 253). 'Peeps' is still a growers' term for the individual flowers of Auriculas and Polyanthuses.

YELLOW LOOSESTRIFE, *Lysimachia vulgaris* (plate 8)

Tall yellow spikes of what Sarah Raven calls 'generous, open-saucer flowers that look straight out at you' made this plant a favourite with Clare, who wanted to see it added to Elizabeth Kent's *Flora Domestica*. As he says, it likes 'splashy places' (NH, 22), and it can still be found by the River Welland, north of Helpston.

SCARLET PIMPERNEL, *Anagallis arvensis* (plate 14)

Clare draws this cornfield weed to the life in *The Shepherd's Calendar*:

>   with its eye of gold
> And scarlet starry points of flowers
> Pimpernel dreading nights and showers
> Oft called 'the shepherds weather glass'
> That sleeps till suns have dryd the grass
> Then wakes and spreads its creeping bloom
> Till clouds or threatning shadows come
> Then close it shuts to sleep again
> Which weeders see and talk of rain
> And boys that mark them shut so soon
> Will call them 'John go bed at noon'   ('May', MP I, 64).

In 'Flower gathering', he alludes to further folklore regarding the pimpernel: girls regard its 'crimson star' as a love-charm –

> And hide it near that witching spot
> Their hearts as herb 'forgetmenot'   (MP II, 102).

EASTERN SOWBREAD, *Cyclamen coum*

We might take Clare's 'Cyclamin flower of a delicate hue' for the pale pink or white blossoms of the autumn-flowering *Cyclamen hederifolium*, were it not for the fact that he includes it in a St Valentine's Day posy along with violets and crocuses ('Valentine' ['The morning is up…'], LP, 406) – which means it can only be the bright pink, spring-flowering *Cyclamen coum*.

Heather family, ERICACEAE

As every gardener knows, plants of this family need acid soil, so we might not expect to find them in a limestone area such as Clare lived in. But much of the higher ground south and west of Helpston was the type of dry grassland called limestone heath, on which lime-loving and lime-hating species grow side by side, the latter in patches of soil from which rainwater, itself mildly acid, has washed out the calcium. The ploughing up of such limestone heath, which began in Clare's day, ruins this delicate ecosystem, and consequently ericaceous plants are now rare in the district.

HEATHER, *Calluna vulgaris*

For Clare this was 'ling' or sometimes, since brooms were made of it, 'besom ling'. It also served as a covert for game birds:

> oft unhousd from beds of ling
> The fluskering pheasant took to wing   ('Hollywell', EP II, 43).

One winter's day the poet dug up a clump of Heather on Helpston Heath and planted it in his garden (NH, 224). If he followed his usual practice of bringing home plenty of the plant's soil, he could have been rewarded with the 'pinky knotts of bloom' that, he tells us, made him love the heath ('The Clump of Fern', MP IV, 307; see p. 20 above). Today he would need to go a little farther afield, to the nature reserve of Castor Hanglands, the only place in Clare's territory where Heather can still be found.

CROSS-LEAVED HEATH, *Erica tetralix*

In his notes on Elizabeth Kent's *Flora Domestica*, Clare describes a plant with leaves in whorls and purple, barrel-shaped flowers that grew on Wittering Heath, to the west of Helpston, 'and no were else in this county' (NH, 19–20, 25); and his ninth Natural History Letter identifies this as the Cross-leaved Heath (NH, 62). According to Druce, Clare could have found it closer to home, on Helpston Heath or Ailsworth Heath. Today, however, it has vanished from the area.

CRANBERRY, *Vaccinium oxycoccos*

In Clare's time, Cranberries trailed plentifully on the brink of Whittlesea Mere, south of Peterborough (NH, 62), but they disappeared after the mere was drained in the middle of the nineteenth century.

Bedstraw family, RUBIACEAE

CLEAVERS and BEDSTRAWS, *Galium* spp.

The hooked bristles that ensure its seeds will be carried off by passing animals – humans included – make Cleavers (meaning 'clingers') by far the best name for what is also called 'goosegrass', *G. aparine*. Clare however knew it by the local name of 'hairiff' or 'hariff'. One of the most moving of his asylum poems recalls the days when he was free to wander and enjoy the sight of Cleavers clambering over unused farm machinery:

> The harrows resting by the hedge
>   The roll within the Dyke
> Hid in the Ariff and the sedge
>   Are things I used to like
>   ('O could I be as I have been...', LP, 653).

Birds' use of Cleavers stalks as nest-building material was something that, in those happier days, Clare recorded in verse and prose ('Birds Nesting', MP II, 172; NH, 117 *et al.*). Two other species, Lady's Bedstraw, *G. verum*, and Hedge Bedstraw, *G. mollugo*, are commended for their beauty in his notes on *Flora Domestica* (NH, 22), and the former's 'countless multitude' of tiny yellow flowers earns it a place in 'Flower gathering' (MP II, 102).

Gentian family, GENTIANACEAE

CENTAURIES, *Centaurium* spp.

Clare rightly describes Common Centaury, *C. erythraea*, and Lesser Centaury, *C. pulchellum*, as 'very pretty' grassland flowers that 'grow in clusters at the top of single stems of a starry form and pink colour with yellow threads in the eyes of them' (NH, 17). The larger species, a biennial wth a rosette of leaves at its base, likes dry grassland and can still be found in some of Clare's haunts. The smaller, an annual with no rosette, needs a damp but open grassy site and, though it is considered extremely rare locally, it can spring up in abundance where the ground is disturbed and grazing is relaxed – conditions that were met in parts of the Castor Hanglands National Nature Reserve during the foot-and-mouth epidemic at the beginning of this century.

YELLOW-WORT, *Blackstonia perfoliata*

Clare must have come across this rather uncommon flower, which is unique among British plants in having eight joined petals, in July 1830 when he included a specimen of it in a basket of wild orchids that he sent Henderson. In his letter of thanks, his friend identified 'the pretty little yellow plant' as Yellow-wort, adding that he had himself found it on Ailsworth Heath 'before Mr French ploughed up the ground'. The plant that Clare sent was probably from Helpston Heath, where Yellow-wort today grows well in the Swaddywell Pit nature reserve.

AUTUMN GENTIAN or FELWORT, *Gentianella amarella* (plate 13)

In a note on Elizabeth Kent's entry for 'Gentian', Clare writes that 'there is a beautiful species of this grows with us of a sort of purple colour or rather fleshy blue' (NH, 19) – a description that best matches Felwort, which brings its distinctive colour to limestone or chalk grassland when nearly all other flowers are finished. Nowadays, in Clare country, it is most likely to be found in a nature reserve such as Barnack Hills and Holes.

Periwinkle family, APOCYNACEAE

PERIWINKLES, *Vinca* spp.

Clare's one brief allusion, a stray couplet in praise of 'The delicate perriwinkle opening blue' ('For the Picturesque', MP II, 210), could have been prompted by plants of either the Lesser Periwinkle, *V. minor*, or the Greater Periwinkle, *V. major*, growing in a garden or naturalised in a wood.

Borage family, BORAGINACEAE

FORGET-ME-NOTS, *Myosotis* spp.

In the early nineteenth century 'forget-me-not' was still a rather bookish name for what were commonly known as 'mouse-ears', from the shape of their leaves, and less commonly as 'scorpion grass', from the curled stalk of their flower-heads. When Clare speaks of the flower's 'tender blue / That gains from poets notice due' ('May', MP I, 64) he may have in mind Coleridge's footnote to his poem 'The Keepsake', urging the adoption of 'forget-me-not' from German. In that language, the name is explained by the story of the knight who, having plucked the flower from the river's edge to please his lady, fell in and was carried away on the current crying '*Vergisz mein nicht!*' But in such lines as

> The mouse ear looked with bright blue eye,
>   And said forget me not
>   ('Flowers and Spring', LP, 318),

Clare's strong sense of the flower's personality brings to mind a less self-consciously romantic explanation of the name. Adam, as he gave a name to each creature in turn, missed out one plant that was quick to protest:

'Forget me not!'

Of the two species that were and remain common in Clare's district, 'the little blue flower aside the brook called in botany water mouse ear' (NH, 287), is the Water Forget-me-not, *M. scorpioides*, while the tender blue flowers uprooted by the party of weeders in *The Shepherd's Calendar* ('May', MP I, 64) must be the Field Forget-me-not, *M. arvensis*, which Druce was calling 'Field Mouse Ear' as late as 1930.

Bindweed family, CONVOLVULACEAE

FIELD BINDWEED, *Convolvulus arvensis*

As a farm worker, Clare must often have struggled with this boa constrictor of a plant, known in Northamptonshire as 'hell weed' and in other Midland counties by the even more expressive name of 'devil's guts'. But he writes pleasurably enough of it as

> trailing bind weed with its pinky cup
> Five lines of paler hue go streaking up
>
> ('The Eternity of Nature', MP III, 530–1).

HEDGE BINDWEED, *Calystegia sepium*

Clare's names for this powerful climber are 'large bindweed bells' in *The Shepherd's Calendar* ('June', MP I, 75), 'convolvulus' in 'Summer Images' (MP III, 152) and 'bell flower' or 'bell bind' in his later poems. Rather confusingly, 'Large Bindweed' is the accepted English name of another species, *C. silvatica*, but this appears to be a comparatively recent introduction, not recorded in Northamptonshire until the twentieth century, though now widespread.

'As white as lillies are in dreams' ('Song' ['The hay was mown...'], LP, 608) is Clare's way of describing the fragile but perfectly shaped blossoms that people in Sussex once simply called 'lilies'. An isolated scrap of verse attempts to capture the way they show up in darkness prior to their rapid wilting:

The gay co[n]volvulus funnel shaped flowers
Look up so eagerly in nights wet hours
And drink so greedy its delicious dew
They seem as drunken to the mornings view
Who sheds her sunny smiles but all in vain
They die for thirst ere evening comes again   (MP II, 224).

Nightshade family, SOLANACEAE

DEADLY NIGHTSHADE, *Atropa belladonna*

Clare must have known this plant, called 'furious and deadly' by Gerard, which is still to be found in old quarries and open sites in his area. But he makes use of it only once, in his first collection of verse, and then as a rather trite metaphor for deception:

The nightshade its blossom is fair to the eye
That harbours dead poison within   ('The Adieu', EP I, 365).

HENBANE, *Hyoscyamus niger*

An account of children's play in the May section of *The Shepherd's Calendar* is enough to make a parent's hair stand on end:

The sitting down when school was oer
Upon the threshold by his door
Picking from mallows sport to please
Each crumpld seed he calld a cheese
And hunting from the stackyard sod
The stinking hen banes velted pod
By youths vain fancys sweetly fed
Christning them his loaves of bread   (MP I, 69).

Can Helpston children *really* have made pretend meals with the fruit of a lethally poisonous plant, source of the hyoscyamine and hyoscine that would one day kill Dr Crippen's wife? The passage's details leave us in no doubt: Henbane does smell unpleasant and its round fruits are protected by a furry calyx. 'Childhood' ('The past is a magic word…', MP III, 237) again tells us that Henbane served for 'loaves of bread'; and though a late poem, also called 'Childhood', speaks reassuringly of nibbled haws substituting for bread-and-butter, it begins with a recollection of Henbane growing close to the church-school at Glinton (LP, 651–2). For Clare that setting always evokes memories of Mary Joyce, and in another asylum poem the thought of his first love transfigures even the sinister-looking Henbane:

> The docks and thistles by the door
> Begemmed by summer showers
> Henbane ne'er looked so bright before
> All might be reckoned flowers
> ('Song' ['At closing day…'], LP, 553).

NIGHTSHADES and POTATO, *Solanum* spp.

Bittersweet, *S. dulcamara*, is alluded to in 'Wild nosegay' when Clare recalls that, as a child, he

> scrambled up the awthorns prickly bower
> For ramping woodbines and blue bitter sweet   (EP II, 384),

a memory that itself turns bitter as the sonnet closes on the 'useless' question: 'When will the feelings come I witnessd then[?]' The name 'bittersweet', however, refers not to the purple-and-yellow flowers but to the poisonous red berries. Mercifully, children who try these spit them out instantly because they are bitter on the palate, although they are said to leave a sweet aftertaste.

It always comes as a surprise to be reminded that the Potato, *S. tuberosum*, is a nightshade. It gets some brief notice in Clare's poetry, and the potatoes grown by his neighbours the Billings brothers figure in his journal as the food plant of the Death's-head Hawk-moth. His friend Henderson highly praised the drawing Clare sent him of this insect. Another survives among the poet's manuscripts.

CHILEAN BOX-THORN, *Vestia foetida*

When Henderson sent Clare plants for his year-old garden at Northborough, he included a specimen of this recent introduction from South America, which he told his friend would grow into a beautiful bush. As depicted in Curtis's *Botanical Magazine* in 1823 (Vol. 50), its clusters of tubular yellow flowers are certainly beautiful, but the unpleasant smell of its evergreen leaves, together with tales of its toxicity, have caused it to remain something of a garden rarity.

Ash family, OLEACEAE

SUMMER JASMINE, *Jasminum officinale*

'Who', asks the seventeenth-century poet Abraham Cowley,

> that has Reason, and his Smell,
> Would not with Roses and with Jasmin dwell?

Certainly Clare would have, whose youthful wish was for a garden with an arbour covered in roses or 'jessamine' ('The Wish', EP I, 46).

ASH, *Fraxinus excelsior*

In one sense, Clare never looked at a tree in his life: what he saw was always a distinct species, and round Helpston it was most likely to be an Ash, still the dominant tree in the area and at the time this is written not yet affected by ash die-back disease. So many shaded the lanes that led south to his favourite hunting-grounds for flowers that he called them 'the ashen groves' ('Cowper Green', EP II, 181). In particular he remembered from his schooldays the 'dear Ash trees' in Glinton churchyard ('Childhood', LP, 651), where he would first have noticed the blackness of ash buds ('Pleasures of Spring', MP III, 49), the glossy bunch-of-keys fruits ('Can I forget…?', LP, 753) and the contrast between the elm's dense foliage and the lighter and light-releasing effect of the 'wing leafed ash' ('The wind suthers softly', LP, 859). Few, however, of the Ash trees that Clare saw would have been left to grow to their full gracefulness: those in woodland were repeatedly coppiced, and the hedgerow ones pollarded, to provide small timber that was malleable in the working but hardened well. A sonnet, 'The Hollow Tree', celebrates one such pollard, an 'Old hugh ash dotterel wasted to a shell' that could shelter ten people (MP IV, 298).

LILAC, *Syringa vulgaris*

When he was growing up Clare knew 'lilac' as the name for *Cardamine pratensis* or Cuckooflower (see p. 96 above). The garden shrub that we now call Lilac then went by the delectable local name of 'prince's feathers' or 'princifeathers', because its arching flower spikes reminded people of the Prince of Wales's crest. And though Clare in 1823 writes of a 'lilac bush' hiding the Village Doctress's door with its flowers (MP III, 342) he reverts to the local name when he laments that village girls no longer gather 'princifeathers cluttering bloom' on May morning ('May', MP I, 73), as he does also when he recalls his boyhood delight at finding 'redcaps' (goldfinches) nesting among the showy blossoms:

> Ive seen them build on eldern boughs
> And tiptop of our russeting   *russet apple tree*
> But never did I see till now
> A birds nest in a garland hing
> In this old princifeather tree
> As hiding it from sudden showers
> The redcaps nest delighteth me
> Snug hid betwixt a bunch of flowers
>   ('Birds Nesting', MP II, 164–5).

In his asylum verse too, Clare uses 'lilac' in songs that he probably wrote on request. But in such a wholly personal poem as 'Childhood' ('O dear to us ever...') he returns to the local name, which his amanuensis William Knight transcribed as 'the old princess-feather tree' (LP, 651).

PRIVETS, *Ligustrum* spp.

Wild Privet, *Ligustrum vulgare*, is a dull shrub to many people, but not to Clare, who relished its lingering autumn colour and the 'rural sweetness' of its scent as it blended with that of Dog-rose and 'woodbine' in summer woodland (NH, 7, 46; 'Summer Evening', EP II, 389). One of his finest poems, 'The Nightingale's Nest', celebrates a thicket known as 'Bushey Close' that was alive with nightingales in spring:

> tis a quiet place
> Thick set with foul royce privet and black thorn   *dogwood*
> So thickly set that birdboys cannot trace
> Its mysteries or climb its little trees
> Unless they creep upon their hands and knees
> As I have crept full many hours away
> To hunt for nests and wood flowers – for in these
> My boyish heart was living...   (MP III, 466).

When Clare began to make a new garden at Northborough, Henderson wrote warning him against planting hedges of Wild Privet because this would not be fully wintergreen and offering instead young plants from the Milton nursery. These would have been of Garden Privet, *L. ovalifolium*.

Slipperwort family, CALCEOLARIACEAE

Molecular evidence has led to a number of genera known to Clare being removed from the once large Figwort family, Scrophulariaceae, and either being added to existing families or placed in 'new' families of which this is one: others are the Speedwell family, Veronicaceae, and the Monkeyflower family, Phrymaceae: see pp. 122–4 and 132–3.

SLIPPERWORT, *Calceolaria* sp.

Cold-shouldered by today's gardeners, in the 1830s Calceolarias had not yet become a feature of garish Victorian 'bedding out' but were still a South American novelty that Lord Milton would have been pleased to display in his flower garden. Henderson sent Clare some young *Calceolaria* plants in July 1833, perhaps in the hope that their strange markings and brilliant colour might help rouse his friend from his despondency.

Speedwell family, VERONICACEAE

See the note on classification before the previous entry.

FOXGLOVES, *Digitalis* spp.

Because the native Foxglove, *D. purpurea*, thrives best on acid soils, it is not easy to find in the woods around Helpston. Clare plays with the fancy that the butterfly he addresses in a youthful poem ('To a Butterfly', EP II, 22) knows thickets where Foxgloves grow. All the same, he urges it to visit the safer refuge of his garden. There it would have found such insect treats as 'the Iron brown fox glove' (NH, 270) – Rusty Foxglove, *D. ferruginea*, a red-brown species from southern and south-eastern Europe which was widely grown in England. Clare spent hours watching leafcutter bees plunder its flowers for pollen – which may help explain why, when he was surrounded by wild Foxgloves in sandy Epping Forest, his thoughts went back to his own garden:

> And there the tall foxglove its red-freckled bell
> To the summer and bee was delicious and dear
> ('I long to forget them…', LP, 14).

It is, however, wild Foxgloves that are remembered in poems written in Northampton Asylum, most notably in the tentative yet haunting lines:

And in the forrest dells
In the midst of solitude
There I hear my lover call
Where the whitethorn forms a wall
And the foxglove blossoms tall
In the tears of eve bedewed

> ('Thy spirit visits me like dew...', LP, 531).

SPEEDWELLS and BROOKLIME, *Veronica* spp.

Britain has over twenty species of these cheerful small flowers. One of the commonest, and the likeliest to have lent its clear blue corolla with the white centre that Clare calls its 'silver eye' ('By all those token flowers ...', LP, 273) to a number of his late love-lyrics, is Germander Speedwell, *V. chamaedrys*. The mention, in a late prose piece, of 'Vernal Speedwell' refers to this rather than to *V. verna*, which is a species found only in the Suffolk Breckland. Another speedwell that he distinguishes by name is the fleshy-stemmed aquatic, Brooklime, *V. beccabunga*, which is pulled out of shallow water by the Village Doctress (MP III, 338). She would have known its proven value as a safeguard against scurvy.

BEARDLIP, *Penstemon barbatus*

A note probably made in September 1826 (NH, 271) shows that the flowers then in bloom in Clare's garden included one that he wrote down as 'Chilome [for Chilone] barbata', which was an early name for *Penstemon barbatus*. This handsome red-flowered species from northern Mexico is recorded as growing at Kew in 1793 – the first of its genus to be introduced into Europe.

SNAPDRAGON, *Antirrhinum majus*

These had been firm favourites since Elizabethan times. 'Snap dragons gaping like to sleepy clowns' stand out among the profusion of cottage garden flowers in the June section of *The Shepherd's Calendar* (MP I, 82).

CLIMBING SNAPDRAGON, *Asarina lophospermum*

This exotic, brilliantly colourful species had only recently come into cultivation in 1833, when Henderson sent Clare a specimen to plant against the wall of his Northborough house. The friends may first have learnt of it from a drawing in Curtis's *Botanical Magazine*, Vol. 57 (1830).

IVY-LEAVED TOADFLAX, *Cymbalaria muralis*
TOADFLAXES, *Linaria* spp.

Elizabeth Kent's entry on Antirrhinums in her *Flora Domestica* reminded Clare that

> there are 2 beautiful speces of 'toad flax' grows wild about us which the common people call 'wild snap dragons' I have found them both the [one] bears bright yellow flowers and the other purple rather smaller the first haunts uncultivated spots by the borders of fields and the other seems fond of old walls and not quite so common as the yellow (NH, 14).

There can be no doubt here that the yellow-flowered plant is the native Common Toadflax, *Linaria vulgaris*, but the purple one is less easy to identify. Clare's description is a close fit for Purple Toadflax, *L. purpurea*, a Tudor introduction which, according to Gent and Wilson, 'must now be in every village growing from pavement cracks or the tops of old walls'. Druce, however, classed it as 'rare' and his 1874 record of it, in the environs of Peterborough, is the first for the Soke; so it is unlikely that it was 'not quite so common as the yellow [toadflax]' fifty years previously. A better case, despite its difference in appearance from other toadflaxes, can be made for that brightener of drab walls, Ivy-leaved Toadflax, *Cymbalaria muralis*. Also an introduction from Italy, it got away to a much better start than *L. purpurea* and was 'common and widely distributed' by Druce's time.

Plantain family, PLANTAGINACEAE

GREATER PLANTAIN, *Plantago major*

The ability to withstand any amount of wear and tear on paths, which makes this plant the enemy of present-day gardeners, was also the reason for its being regarded over many centuries with near-reverence as a herb that could heal any kind of injury. In fact its crushed leaves are a styptic, as the children gathering Cowslips for their May Day cuckaballs knew ('Sport in the Meadows', MP III, 452). Clare is characteristically aware too of its usefulness to other forms of life. Goldfinches feed on its seeds (NH, 44) and its broad leaves shelter a variety of smaller creatures:

> And full often drowning wet
> Scampering beetles rac'd away
> Safer shelter glad to get
> Drownded out from whence they lay
> While the moth for nights reprief
> Waited safe and snug withall
> Neath the plantains bowery leaf
> Where there neer a drop coud fall
>   ('Recollections after a Ramble', EP II, 193).

Figwort family, SCROPHULARIACEAE

MULLEINS, *Verbascum* spp.

At one stage in the composition of 'The Village Doctress', 'mullin growing to a mighty size' figured among the herbs gathered by Clare's wisewoman (MP III, 338). This would have been Great Mullein, *V. thapsus*, a handsome plant that can attain human height. Clare himself scored a botanical 'first' for the area when he recorded 'antique mullins flannel leaves' among the vegetation of Cowper Green (EP II, 183) – 'antique' presumably referring to the white-haired effect of the plant's felted leaves. After describing the plant, which he says was locally known as 'goldilocks', in one of his natural history letters, he goes on to say that it was a rarity of the district that botanists would come miles to gather (NH, 62). This is puzzling, since *V. thapsus* was, and remains, easy to find in the Helpston area: perhaps Clare misunderstood a description by one of these botanists of Moth Mullein, *V. blattaria*, a very rare introduced species that has been recorded in the Soke.

Another uncommon species, 'nothing like the flannel Mullin', he believed to grow only near Barnack, to the west of Helpston. He describes it in careful detail at the end of his commentary on Elizabeth Kent's book:

> … the vulgar call it 'Sweet Mullin' from the violet scent of its flowers – its leaves are exactly like the fox glove and its flowers grow on stalks like soldiers feathers or the double larkheel as thick as they can stand by each other of a bright yellow with purple threads in the middle (NH, 23).

This is Dark Mullein, *V. nigrum* (plate 12), to the life. Happily, it can still be found at several places in the district.

WATER FIGWORT, *Scrophularia auriculata*

Clare calls this 'water betony', which until very recently was its common English name. One of the plants that Hermann Müller in his pioneer work on pollination was to label 'wasp flowers', it was already 'wasp weed' to Clare's gipsy friends (*By Himself*, 85). There is however no basis for Clare's belief that wasps got from it a comb-building material, nor for the gipsies' belief that it cured deafness.

Dead-nettle family, LAMIACEAE

Ground flora though most members of this family may be, its typical species can always make their presence felt. They achieve this by being strongly aromatic, by spreading runners in all directions, and by lifting whorls of wide-lipped, colourful flowers, tiered like a wedding cake, on sturdy square stems. The family was previously known as Labiatae, in reference to the lipped flowers.

HEDGE WOUNDWORT, *Stachys sylvatica*

'A Woodland Seat' is a poem about the overlooked beauty of two common weeds, Dandelions and a 'nettle', of which Clare says

> kings cannot wear
> Robes prankt with half the splendour of a flower
> Pencilled with hues of workmanship divine (MP IV, 245).

Clearly this is not a Stinging Nettle but one of those members of the Lamiaceae that are popularly called nettles because of their triangular toothed leaves. The commonest of these, and the one that Clare, according to Anne Baker's *Glossary*, knew as the 'wild-grass nettle', is Hedge Woundwort, which has a purple corolla 'pencilled' with white markings. The lighter-coloured Marsh Woundwort, *S. palustris*, is another possibility, but it is far less common round Helpston; it does however hybridise with the commoner species.

BETONY, *Betonica officinalis* (plate 11)

In apostrophising Cowper Green where he found so many wild flowers, Clare writes that 'medicinal betony / By thy wood side railing reeves' (EP II, 183). Medicinal it was certainly held to be at the time: Hill's *Family Herbal*, which Clare owned, says it is 'of very great virtue'. 'Reeves', meaning 'winds' or 'bends', may refer to the way the plant spreads by putting out runners. The flower itself does not bend, but has an erect, purple-clad dignity that Edward Thomas captured in August 1914 when he noticed – also at the edge of a wood –

A sentry of dark betonies,
The stateliest of small flowers on earth.

YELLOW ARCHANGEL, *Lamiastrum galeobdolon*
DEAD-NETTLES, *Lamium* spp.

I have put these together because the White Dead-nettle, *Lamium album*, and the Red Dead-nettle, *Lamium purpureum*, were also sometimes called Archangels. Clare could have had any or all of them in mind when he jotted down a protest at the name: 'I suppose that the dead nettle had the good fortune to get [k]nighted with the fine title of "Archangel" by some poet of this "golden age" and the nettle ought to be thankful for his lordships pastoral condesencion' (NH, 51). In fact the name, for which there is no satisfactory explanation, had been used by English herbalists for a thousand years or more.

All three plants deserved the poet's notice, but there is only one brief mention of Red and White Dead-nettles, in some tentative lines beginning 'The red bagged bee' (LP, 177).

WHITE HOREHOUND, *Marrubium vulgare*

One of Clare's most botanical poems, 'Cowper Green', surveys the plants that grew on this expanse of grassland: first those he considered weeds, then wild flowers, and finally herbs in the everyday sense of plants used for flavouring. Among these last, the leaves of 'horehound tufts' (EP II, 183) would have stood out by reason of their covering of fine white hairs. A native of the south and west of Britain, in the Soke it can only have been the relic of a garden herb that at the time was still being grown to provide the basis for a cough cure or as flavouring for the 'Sweet candied horehound cakes' sold in village shops ('August', MP I, 121). Now however it is thought to be locally extinct.

BUGLE, *Ajuga reptans*

The wonderfully strong blue of its flowers and its tolerance of woodland shade are what distinguish this plant for Clare ('Cowper Green', EP II, 183; 'The Wild-flower Nosegay', EP II, 410). An allusion to 'the bugles rattle flowers' ('The Bonny Maple Tree', LP, 922) is perplexing, because the blue

Bugle's seeds produce no sound when the plant is shaken. However, Bugle was once known in Wiltshire as 'baby rattle', a name that could conceivably be based on a fancied resemblance in the shape of Bugle flowers to those of the Yellow-rattle – which in fact (see p. 133) belongs to the Broomrape family.

SELFHEAL, *Prunella vulgaris*

To many people today this is a tiresome intruder in their lawns, but to Clare's Woodman it is a 'wonderous' cure for the wounds that are his occupational hazard ('The Woodman' ['The beating snow…'], EP II, 292). It is for this reason that the Village Doctress gathers 'self heal flowering in a russet husk' (MP III, 337), the husk being the bushy brown calyx; Clare tells us that the gipsies' name for the plant was 'husk head' (*By Himself*, 85).

BALM, *Melissa officinalis*

This fragrant garden herb which, according to a medieval herbalist quoted by Culpeper, 'causeth heart and mind to become merry', is also known as 'lemon balm' or 'bee balm'. What attracts bees to it is not its nectar, which their tongues cannot reach, but an oil in its leaves produced by substances that also make up the Nasonov pheromone that enables a worker bee to attract other workers back to the colony. Clare's Village Doctress knew nothing of pheromones, but she did know that rubbing her new hives with lemon balm leaves would encourage swarming bees to settle in them (MP III, 339). Today's beekeepers instead use a synthetic lure consisting of citral and geraniol in a 2:1 ratio. See also 'Fennel' (pp. 156–7).

BASIL THYME, *Clinopodium acinos*

'[P]ennyroyals creeping twine', which occurs among other herbs in the early poem 'Cowper Green' (EPII, 183), is unlikely to be Pennyroyal, *Mentha pulegium*, because that is a very rare plant of damp habitats whereas the spot that Clare is describing is a sandy area of short turf that has once been quarried – 'Here a knowl and there a scoop' (EPII, 184).

But the name 'Pennyroyal' was sometimes used of other members of the Dead-nettle family, and Druce decided that the low-spreading and aromatic Basil Thyme was the plant here meant. See, however, the entry for 'Mints and Pennyroyal' on p. 131.

HYSSOP, *Hyssopus officinalis*

This is not the plant of which the name is translated as 'hyssop' in the King James Bible, but a one-time favourite of the herb garden with a variety of uses – as pot herb, strewing herb, ingredient of perfumes and liqueurs, and medicine. Two manuscripts of 'The Village Doctress' contain an additional stanza in which Clare names Hyssop as one of the herbs in her garden (MP III, 345). She is most likely to have cut its handsome blue flower-spikes in order to make an infusion that would relieve coughs and colds.

WILD MARJORAM, *Origanum vulgare*

Clare called this widely-gathered native herb 'doubly sweet' ('Cowper Green', EP II,183) either in reference to its taste and smell or to the fact that leaves and flowers alike have a pleasant taste. In his poem 'Flower gathering', a passing milkmaid tucks a sprig of it into her dress, in the hopeful belief that it

> makes the swain
> Amourous to kiss her oer again   (MP II, 102).

THYMES, *Thymus* spp.

In a number of poems Clare writes about the pleasure of sitting on a hillock covered in sweet-scented Wild Thyme, *T. polytrichus* (plate 14). He believed that such hillocks were thrown up by moles, and even addresses a sonnet to their 'Rude architect' ('The Mole', MP IV, 294). If he occasionally alludes to 'pismire hills', it is because he thought of the red ants seen running about these mounds as tenants of the mole's earthworks.

The truth of the matter of course is that ants, though of a different species – the small yellow meadow ant – are responsible for the heaps of fine, compacted soil which are a favourite habitat of Wild Thyme and one that it often shares with Common Rock-rose, as Clare remembers in a late lyric ('Do ye like the Heath, Lassie?', LP, 1019). He would also have known several varieties of Garden Thyme, *Thymus vulgaris*, including the 'silver thyme' mentioned in 'The Cross Roads' (EP II, 628).

MINTS and PENNYROYAL, *Mentha* spp.

One of Clare's late lyrics conjures up the herbal scents round a cottage door:

> Love come the back way in By the Mint and lads love tree
> ('Come the back way dear', LP 886).

The mint is most likely to have been the introduced Spear Mint, *M. spicata*, though Clare tells us that the native Water Mint, *M. aquatica*, was planted in cottage gardens 'were it looses its rankness and has a very pleasant smell and gets the name of "Mint of life"' (NH, 21). Rankness such as has been compared to that of a ripe Gorgonzola cheese is also a feature of Corn Mint, *M. arvensis*, which Clare knew as 'horse mint'

> that steaming goes
> When trod upon strong up the ploughmans nose
> ('Tis morn…', MP V, 50).

Another labiate with a pungent scent that Clare remembered in later life was Pennyroyal, *M. pulegium*. In 'Bonny Jenny-O' (LP, 805) it makes an appearance 'pinheaded o'er wi' dew', a description that fits the clustered flowers of this rare plant better than it does the sparser ones of Basil Thyme, a plant that Clare also knew as 'Pennyroyal' (see pp. 129–30).

132

SCARLET BERGAMOT, *Monarda didyma*

Whereas all Clare's other labiates are of European origin, here is one that has the distinction of having been discovered on the shore of Lake Ontario in 1744 by John Bartram. The handsome flower-heads rising pagoda-fashion, one above the other, soon made it a cottage garden favourite: 'I think you have plenty of Monarda didyma – the scarlet bergamot – I wish you would send me a plant', Henderson wrote to Clare in the autumn of 1831.

LAVENDER, *Lavandula angustifolia*

Lavender, according to *The Shepherd's Calendar* ('June', MP I, 82), is to be found in every cottage garden because it is the 'choice of every lass': witness the one who 'nips a leaf of lavender / To put within her gown' ('Summer Ballad', MP IV, 143).

SWEET BASIL, *Ocimum basilicum*

In a note that was probably made in August 1826, Clare records his observation that hive bees foraging in a border of various herbs kept to the same species of plant: some of them 'searched the tufts of Basil and interfered with no other untill they had gathered their loads and winged their way home to their hives' (NH 270).

SAGE, *Salvia officinalis*

As its botanical name suggests, this was once thought of as a life-saving plant as well as a common culinary herb – 'Why should a man die when he has sage?' But in the verse tale, 'The Cross Roads', Jane kills herself, her mother dies of grief, and weeds replace the sage and other herbs that once grew in their now derelict garden (EP II, 628).

Monkeyflower family, PHRYMACEAE

This is another newly defined family, bringing together, as the result of recent molecular evidence, a number of genera hitherto placed in the Figwort family, Scrophulariaceae.

MUSK, *Mimulus moschatus*

The 'tufts of smelling musk' that grow in the ideal garden Clare describes in an early poem, 'The Wish' (EP I, 47), must be *Mimulus moschatus*, introduced from North America in the previous century. Clare's wish was granted on his thirty-second birthday, 13 July 1825, when Henderson promised him a present of various plants including 'the Monkey Flower' (NH, 250), unless this was the more handsome *M. guttatus*.

Broomrape family, OROBANCHACEAE

Both the genera below are partly parasitic plants that as a result of recent molecular investigations have been transferred here from the Figwort family, Scrophulariaceae.

COMMON EYEBRIGHT, *Euphrasia nemorosa* (plate 6)

Of the many species of eyebright distinguished by botanists, *E. nemorosa*, recorded (under its earlier name of *E. curta*) by Druce as growing on Helpston Heath, seems the most likely to have been the 'famous eye brights' with 'slightly penciled flowers' that Clare's Village Doctress gathered in the belief that it was 'Infallible for weak short sighted eyes' (MP III, 338).

YELLOW-RATTLE, *Rhinanthus minor*

A late lyric, 'To Julia', is addressed to a real young woman called Julia Wiggington who lived in Northampton and Clare pictures her in a realistic setting of flowers in bloom at haymaking time – knapweed, Meadowsweet, Salad Burnet,

And rattles like a pencil case
That sound and rattles in the hand   (LP, 914).

In his 1930 flora, Druce described the Yellow-rattle as 'too abundant'.

Today, herbicides are used to prevent it lessening the grass content of the hay by weakening the grasses on which it is hemiparasitic. But conservationists, trying here and there to restore a meadow to its former glory, deliberately sow Yellow-rattle for two reasons: to give wild flowers and the more delicate grasses a chance to replace the plant's weakened hosts, and – most importantly – to give their children the joy of shaking the dried pods and hearing the seeds rattle inside.

Bladderwort family, LENTIBULARIACEAE

COMMON BUTTERWORT, *Pinguicula vulgaris*

Clare's untitled lines beginning 'The rank luxuriant Flag…' contrast two streamside flowers: the showy Yellow Iris and the Common Butterwort, whose

> blue eye
> Shaped like the violet doth so hidden lye
> That een the botanist much less the clown
> Wins not its glances till he stoops adown
> To pay it notice and as in amaze
> It seems to shrink in grass to shun his praise   (MP II, 313).

No wonder botanists sought it out: Common Butterwort, so called, was rare as far south as the Helpston area, where, in an SSSI, one tiny colony survives in just such a watery setting as Clare gives it in this fragment. It was more familiar to the northerner Wordsworth, who wrote an enthusiastic description of it in the margin of his copy of a widely used flora. One wonders what he and Clare made of the insects stuck to the leaves of this graceful and delicate-looking small plant, which is now known to be carnivorous.

Indian Bean family, BIGNONIACEAE

CHILEAN GLORYFLOWER, *Eccremocarpus scaber*

Henderson included this in a consignment of plants he sent to Clare in 1833 in the hope – 'Let me hear from you by the bearer...' – that they would rouse his friend from a long silence induced by depression. A rapid climber, it was intended, as was the Climbing Snapdragon that he sent with it (see p. 124), for the south-facing wall of Clare's cottage.

Vervain family, VERBENACEAE

VERVAIN, *Verbena officinalis*

Described by Clare as a 'little plant with a hard stem that grows in villages and waste places' and bears minute purple flowers (*By Himself*, 85), Vervain for centuries had great significance among herbalists as a supposed cure for numerous diseases, including 'the king's evil', scrofula. Clare learnt its name, which he spells 'burvine', from gipsies encamped in Helpston parish – one of the districts of the Soke where this plant can still be found. See also p. 98.

Holly family, AQUILIFOLIACEAE

HOLLY, *Ilex aquifolium*

It comes as a surprise to discover that, in the Soke, Holly is nearly always a planted shrub of churchyards and gardens, and not the indigenous component of the landscape that it is in much of Britain. Clare welcomes the shelter it gives in a garden ('The holly bush...', MP V, 225) but seems to think of it chiefly as a Christmas decoration, in which context the 'Gilt holly' of 'December' (MP I, 157) suggests – since there were no gilding spray-guns in his day – a variegated green-and-gold garden variety.

Bellflower family, CAMPANULACEAE

BELLFLOWERS and HAREBELL, *Campanula* spp.

Bellflowers come in all sizes. Clare confuses the two tall native species when, in his notes on *Flora Domestica*, he identifies the 'wild stalking canterbury bell' of 'Wild-flower Nosegay' as Elizabeth Kent's Giant Throatwort – 'throatworts' being the herbalists' name for bellflowers. Giant Bellflower, *C. latifolia*, does occur in the Soke, but as a northern plant it is near its south-eastern limit, and the rather shorter Nettle-leaved Bellflower, *C. trachelium*, which is a southern species, is much more likely to be met with in ancient woodland near Helpston; among a number of records Druce includes his own discovery of it in Hilly Wood.

Clare's notes on *Flora Domestica* also allude to a less tall bellflower growing on 'hilly ground', which Grainger identifies as Clustered Bellflower, *C. glomerata* (plate 12). As we might expect, it is now as rare as the unimproved grassland on which it once grew. He also mentions two garden bellflowers of European origin: Peach-leaved Bellflower, *C. persicifolia*, which he mistakenly thinks is one of the native species renamed, and a white variety of the familiar Canterbury-bells, *C. medium* (NH, 15). Compared with the more or less erect flowers of the native species, the flowers of this last hang down a little when fully open, as Clare remembered many years later:

> Wi' hairy leaves and dro[o]ping flowers The canterberry bell
> Grows underneath [the] hazle bower
> ('The Evening is for Love', LP, 742).

Elizabeth Kent goes on to describe the smallest of British bellflowers, *C. rotundifolia* (plate 11), known today as Harebell (in Scotland, Bluebell). Clare's problem with this is not one of recognition but of nomenclature. He had grown up calling the woodland Bluebell of spring, *Hyacinthoides non-scripta*, 'harebell' and in his early poetry he has no specific name for 'the little bell flowers' that lingered on open grassland late in the year ('Written in November', EP II, 337). By the time he read *Flora Domestica* he knew them by the name that Elizabeth Kent favours, 'heath bells' (meaning 'heather bells'), but this, he complains, does not go well into metre, and he is more attracted by another of her names, 'harvest bells', which he uses twice in his 1824 journal (NH, 193, 199). In his poetry, however, Harebells continue to be 'heath bells': in 'The Thrush's Nest', for example, the bird's eggs are 'like heath bells gilt with dew' (MP IV, 187).

GARDEN LOBELIA, *Lobelia erinus*

Lobelia would have been the most familiar to Clare of the half-hardy or tender plants that Henderson sent him in July 1833 for bedding out in his Northborough garden. It had been introduced from the Cape of Good Hope as long ago as the seventeenth century.

Bogbean family, MENYANTHACEAE

BOGBEAN, *Menyanthes trifoliata*

Bogbean, 'shining in its mozzly dyes', was gathered as a medicinal herb by Clare's Village Doctress (MP III, 337) and also by his gipsy friends. The fact that his father was crippled by rheumatism may well have alerted the poet to the plant's pain-relieving power. It has become very rare in Clare country, but its beautifully fringed, pink-and-white flowers may be found in a boggy, out-of-the-way spot.

Daisy family, ASTERACEAE

Among the most highly evolved of the dicotyledons, the 'starry' family is the great success story of the plant world. By spreading a large number of florets over inviting, pizza-shaped flower-heads (whence the former name of Compositae), and by developing a slow-release mechanism for the florets' pollen, many of its members have ensured that pollination by a variety of insects goes on for a week or more. And the safe dispersal of a floret's single seed is more often than not effected by a tiny parachute (pappus) of fine hairs, evolved from the calyx. To crown it all some species have even 'learnt' (actually, of course, been selected) to mimic more successful ones, thus making difficulties for the botanist.

BURDOCKS, *Arctium* spp.

Burdock leaves provided Helpston children with tablecloths for their pretend feasts ('Childhood', MP III, 237) and their village wisewoman with an ingredient for her potions ('The Village Doctress, MP III, 337). The plants were however best known for the clinging fruits that are said to have inspired the creation of Velcro. In 'Valentine Eve', a girl's attempt to remove them from her skirt prompts her lover to declare his feelings–

> Mary theres one whose thoughts when your away
> Always cling with you full as close as they
> Who hopes yet fears his growing love to name
> Lest you should throw it from you just the same   (MP III, 73).

The burdocks met with on these footpath rambles are likely to have been Lesser Burdock, *Arctium minus*. In 'Farewell', a haunting poem about Clare's memories of a water mill, its owner and his three daughters that was written in Northampton at a time when he was confined to the asylum, the rather less common Greater Burdock, *A. lappa*, is recalled in the line: 'I' the neak the large burdock Grows near the green willow' (LP, 730). Druce thought that by 'large burdock' Clare must mean Butterbur, *Petasites hybridus*. But *A. lappa* often grows by water; 'large' is usually a specifying word with Clare (as with 'large bindweed bells': see p. 116); and he is unlikely to have mistaken an untidy mass of Butterbur for the structured and handsome Greater Burdock that landscape artists of the period loved to paint.

THISTLES, *Cirsium* spp.

In May 1820 Clare composed, to the rhythm of his mother's spinning wheel, the song that begins

> Swamps of wild rush beds and sloughs squashy traces
> Grounds of rough fallow wi thistle and weed…
> > ('Song', EP II, 100).

'Rough fallow' became a reality again for late twentieth-century readers when the European Agricultural Commission began to subsidise farmers for set-aside land. In no time at all thistles, thanks to their marvellous seed-dispersal mechanism, '[s]pread families around' – as Clare puts it in 'The Labourer's Passing Sigh' (EP II, 200). For goldfinches this meant bonanzas of the kind described in Clare's prose writings, where they descend in flocks to feed on thistle seeds or to pull off last year's down for the distinctive lining of their nests (NH, 44).

The wild places of Clare's spinning song reappear in a letter he wrote over thirty years later:

> while other people are looking at gay flower Gardens – I love to see the quaking bullrushes and the broad Lakes in the green meadows – and the sheep tracks over a fallowfield and a Land of thistles in flower.

Now, however, he is 'in this d—d mad house and cant get out' (*Letters*, 680). His anger suggests that he has been going through a bad patch, perhaps one of those periods when, in an attempted Scots dialect, he extolled the warrior thistle as symbol of defiance and liberty. But before mental illness closed in upon him, Clare had written a very different poem in celebration of a single 'hugh [huge] thistle spurred with many thorns' as the heavily-defended refuge for various forms of wildlife – smaller plants, insects and such ground-nesting birds as the peewit, yellowhammer, corn bunting and partridge (MP V, 203). Edmund Blunden was the first to print this splendid and thoroughly ecological poem, and the first to give it a title identifying its subject as Spear Thistle, *Cirsium vulgare*, which Clare elsewhere calls 'the very whasp of flowers' ('The Fear of Flowers', MP IV, 284).

In another poem, 'Forrest Flowers', the 'Star pointed thistle with its ruddy flowers' (MP IV, 274) is identified by Druce as Marsh Thistle, *C. palustre*, presumably because this species can occur in damp woodland, whereas the thistle cut from the wheat by the weeding party in 'May' of *The Shepherd's Calendar* (MP I, 63) would be Creeping Thistle, *C. arvense*, called 'a great agricultural pest' by Druce.

KNAPWEEDS and CORNFLOWER, *Centaurea* spp.

Clare finds the perfect image for Common Knapweed, *C. nigra*, in the shaving-brush-like topknot worn by the lead horse of a team: 'button knapweed with its blossom threads / Nobs like red toppings on fore horses heads' ('Valentine Eve', MP III, 77, variant). Girls in his village played a divination game with these purple-red 'threads', which are the columns of joined anthers that project from the tiny florets once they have opened. They would strip them from a flower-head of Common Knapweed or 'hardheads', *C. nigra*, and tuck the remaining knob between their breasts. If, after an hour or so, any of the next inner ring of florets had opened and revealed its anthers, this was a sure sign that the girl had a seriously-intentioned lover (MP I, 66). (One presumes the sudden warmth had the effect of prematurely opening florets that were programmed to open the next day.)

Helpston girls would not have had far to look for Common Knapweed, which Clare also calls 'knob weed' and 'iron weed'. As tough as the latter name implies, it can grow anywhere –

> content to share
> The meanest spot that spring can spare
> Een roads were danger hourly comes   *where*
> Is not wi out its purple blooms
>
> ('May', MP I, 63).

By contrast, the handsome Greater Knapweed, *C. scabiosa* (plate 13), with its crown-of-thorns outer circle of florets, prefers an open and upland grassy site and so is likely to be the species Clare refers to as 'knob weeds blood red on the hill' ('Song' ['The cows they are out…'], LP, 933). Druce classed Greater Knapweed as 'locally common' in Northamptonshire in general and 'abundant' at Helpston in particular, but the 2012 *Flora of Northamptonshire* says it is now limited for the most part to verges and blames this on the ploughing up of grassland.

A much worse fate has befallen another member of the genus, Cornflower, *C. cyanus* (plate 14). A weed of cultivation, and so at the mercy of seed cleansing and herbicides, it was already 'declining' in Clare country when Druce published his *Flora* in 1930 and is now almost extinct throughout the British Isles except where sown in wild-flower mixtures. Cornflower blue, the colour that Clare praises whenever he writes about the 'blue caps' or 'corn bottles' that 'Eddie like Butterflies' as the wind passes over green wheat ('Song' ['The hurley, burly wind ...'], LP, 605), is today mainly a term in the dress trade. We have to make do with growing our Cornflowers in the mixed border – perhaps alongside Sweet Sultan, *C. moschata*, a favourite of cottage gardeners and allegedly of the Grand Turk himself, to which Clare makes a passing allusion as 'the sultan with its husky flowers' ('Beautiful Maria', LP, 736).

CHICORY, *Cichorium intybus*

Clare's poetry affords us a glimpse or two of Chicory, which he calls 'endive' – 'That steals its colors from the sky' ('The Last of Summer', MP II, 54; see also 'My bonny Sue', LP, 769). This pure intense blue has led to its having been identified as the original Blue Flower, the Romantic poets' symbol of the unattainable: an image lived up to in the flashes of colour we sometimes catch sight of as we speed down a recently built road. These may be the result of Chicory's liking for bare, disturbed ground, although the deliberate sowing of seed from a cultivated strain is a more probable explanation.

HAWKBITS, *Scorzoneroides autumnalis* and *Leontodon hispidus*

'Look over the gap in that hedge', Clare says to his companion on 'A Walk in the Fields',

                    and behold
    The closes that seem to be litterd wi gold
    Tis the hawk weed in blossom some deem it a weed
    And feth I must own it looks simple indeed
    When found by itself but in summers fine weather
    You see what a show they make blowing together
                                        (MP III, 377).

Today, 'hawkweed' is the accepted English name for the genus *Hieracium*, but in Clare's time the name appears to have been used also for hawkbits and since these are much more common in the Soke than are hawkweeds we can assume them to be the flowers in this passage. 'Litterd' certainly brings to mind the way that disks of intense gold appear all over a meadow when the flower-heads, which close in bad weather, open in response to summer sunshine. As Rough Hawkbit, *Leontodon hispidus*, shares a long flowering season with the Autumn Hawkbit, *Scorzoneroides autumnalis* (formerly called *Leontodon autumnalis*), either species could have provided this show, just as either could be the 'hawkweed flowers' of the late love lyric 'Oh! bonny is the country', which starts "'Tis Autumn' (LP, 763).

SOWTHISTLES, *Sonchus* spp.

Whether Smooth Sowthistle, *S. oleraceus*, or Prickly Sowthistle, *S. asper*, these plants are to most people simply the weediest of weeds. But, though Clare's few allusions to them in his asylum poems fall short of D. H. Lawrence's declaration that the flowering of *Sonchus* is a manifestation of the Holy Ghost, the line 'The milky sowthistles their pale tops I kiss' ('In the field', LP, 839) registers his pleasure in the yellow flowers topping the plant's latex-charged stems.

DANDELIONS, *Taraxacum* microspecies

Fully open in sunshine – or, as Clare puts it in a bit of Byronic rhyme-play, 'with the suns warm eye on' – the Dandelion is seen as a miniature sun in 'A Rhapsody' (LP, 995). But later in the same stanza its flowers have 'closed like painters brush when evening was': an image that brings to mind the furled Dandelions painted three hundred years earlier by Dürer in his 'Large Piece of Turf'.

PLOUGHMAN'S-SPIKENARD, *Inula conyzae* (plate 12)

Clare found this rather dingy herb with the 'spicey smell' that accounts for its name (nard being a costly Indian perfume) on Cowper Green

(EP II, 183). Today's distribution maps show that the plant, though uncommon, continues to grow in a number of places in the Soke.

COMMON FLEABANE, *Pulicaria dysenterica*

In 'A Walk', written not long after his move to Northborough in 1832, Clare sets out to explore his new surroundings and discovers that the fenland landscape is far from being uniformly 'dreary'. One of the first things to catch his eye is

> a sloping bank profusely spread
> With yarrow ragwort fleabane all in flower
> As showy almost as a garden bed   (MP IV, 312).

The interest of this is that Druce, who would not have known this poem, gives Northborough as one of the places where this attractive flower with the unattractive name could be found in his day.

CANADIAN GOLDENROD, *Solidago canadensis*

Said to be the first plant to be introduced into Britain from the New World, what we now call Canadian Goldenrod was brought from Virginia in 1648 by the younger Tradescant. By the time Clare was grown up, however, gardeners were consigning it to the compost heap – less, one suspects, because it was out of fashion, than through exasperation with its invasiveness:

> golden rods and tanzey running high
> That oer the pail tops smild on passers bye
> Flowers in my time that every one woud praise
> Tho thrown like weeds from gardens now adays
> ('The Cross Roads', EP II, 628).

MICHAELMAS-DAISIES, *Aster* spp.

'The Michaelmass daisey is in full flower', Clare wrote in his journal on 20 October 1824,

> both the lilac-blue and the white thick set with its little clustering stars of flowers I love them for their visits in such a mellancholy season as the end of autumn (NH, 193).

In verse these become, in lines possibly intended for 'November' in *The Shepherd's Calendar*, 'The large one shining wi its lilac stars' and 'tother wi its tiny mozzling flowers' (MP I, 154). By Clare's time so many American species of *Aster* had become naturalised in Britain, and so many garden varieties had been developed here, that it is impossible to put names to the two which raised his spirits at Helpston.

CHINA ASTER, *Callistephus chinensis*

To most of us these are the cheerful mop-heads of small gardens, but at a time when Clare was depressed and debilitated they seemed to him, for all their 'pied lustre of red white and blue', to bend in a brooding silence before the approach of autumn (NH, 175).

DAISY, *Bellis perennis*

'Welcome old Maytey' are Clare's opening words of 'To an April Daisy' (EP I, 135). Like any good mate it can be relied upon to turn up when expected. So when the poet writes of 'The Eternity of Nature', the Daisy is his prime example:

> Its little golden bosom frilled with snow
> Might win een eve to stoop adown and show
> Her partner Adam in the silky grass
> This little gem that smiled where pleasure was

– and because it loved Eve in return, it carried its gift of giving pleasure into the fallen world, with the result that

> When eighteen hundred years our common date
> Grows many thousands in their marching state
> Aye still the child with pleasure in his eye
> Shall cry the daisy a familiar cry
> And run to pluck it   (MP III, 528).

Clare also pays passing notice to garden daisies, whether of the scarlet and white kind that he grew himself ('Rural Evening', EP II, 640; NH, 217) or the double kind known as 'Bess in her bravery' ('June', MP I, 82). But these are mere varieties of the one-and-only native Daisy, characterised by its 'golden eye and silver rim with its delicate blushing stains underneath' (*By Himself*, 53), that blossoms in real-life profusion throughout Clare's poetry.

TANSY, *Tanacetum vulgare*

Despite its past medicinal importance, Tansy is still being thrown out of gardens, as it was in Clare's lifetime (see the quotation under 'Canadian Goldenrod' on p. 143), with the result that a plant considered 'rare' by Druce a century ago is now scattered throughout Northamptonshire, the Helpston area included.

MUGWORT, SOUTHERNWOOD and WORMWOOD, *Artemisia* spp.

In Epping Forest, at the time he was a patient in Dr Allen's asylum, Clare listened to a nightingale singing 'Where mugwort grows like mignonette' ('To the Nightingale', LP, 16). This comparison of Mugwort, *A. vulgaris* – a rather bedraggled-looking herb for all its reputed medicinal value – with an elegant garden plant suggests that Clare wants us to know that his nightingale, unlike Keats's, sings in real country, not among musk roses in a Hampstead garden.

There is, however, a garden mugwort, Southernwood or, to Clare, 'ladslove' (see also p. 42), *A. abrotanum*, which Helpston girls included in their clipping-posies on account of its strong and lingering smell ('June', MP I, 82). It was this that caused it to be planted near cottage doors: a fact Clare alludes to in a late lyric ('Come the back way dear', LP, 886) and that Edward Thomas makes the theme of one of his finest poems, 'Old Man' (another name for the herb), in which he watches his daughter pick and crumble the leaves:

And I can only wonder how much hereafter
She will remember, with that bitter scent,
Of garden rows, and ancient damson-trees
Topping a hedge, a bent path to a door,
A low thick bush beside the door, and me
Forbidding her to pick.

With its silver leaves and spikes of bobbing yellow flowers, the medicinal herb Wormwood, *A. absinthium*, is a handsome member of the genus. In Clare's day it must have been profuse enough on the heaths south of Helpston for him to write of 'wormwood hills which many a play endeared' ('The joys of childhood...', EP II, 525). He also associated it with waste places, where it consorted with burdocks and Henbane that had likewise been 'Driven like rebels from the culturd soil' ('Spring' ['How beautiful the spring'], MP III, 35). Whether dug out by farmers or sold – very profitably, it is recorded – to London herbalists, it had become rare in the Soke by Druce's time, although it still persists there in a few places.

LAVENDER-COTTON, *Santolina chamaecyparissus*

Two allusions in Clare's late poetry suggest that he first met the grey foliage and small yellow flowers of the garden shrub Santolina, as it is now generally called, in the garden of the Northampton Asylum ('A Valentine', LP, 301; 'The Ladybird', LP 762).

YARROWS, *Achillea* spp.

Grateful for its presence in the sombre fenland landscape, Clare, in the late summer following his move to Northborough, devoted a sonnet to the 'dark leaves like to clumps of little ferns' and the 'swarms of flowers… Some blushing into pink and others white' that are distinctive of Yarrow, *A. millefolium* ('The Yarrow', MP IV, 324). In his Helpston garden he had grown a yellow kind, which was probably Fern-leaf Yarrow, *A. filipendulina* (NH, 214, 225).

CHRYSANTHEMUMS, *Glebionis segetum* and *Chrysanthemum* spp.

In his notes on *Flora Domestica*, Clare writes that our native chrysanthemum, the Corn Marigold (now *Glebionis segetum*, since it has been deprived of its rightful generic name), 'is in great plenty with us and reckond a troublesome weed the common people call them "golds"' (NH, 18). This country name, which is the one used by William and Dorothy Wordsworth, also appears in verses that recall 'the wheat-field where the blue-cap grew / With crimson corn-flowers and the yellow gould' ('Elegy', EP I, 121). Unlike the doomed blue-caps, 'goulds' persist in Clare's neighbourhood, although they arc now classed as rare weeds.

  The autumn of 1824 was so mild that at the end of November Henderson was able to send Clare sample blooms of seven new garden varieties of *Chrysanthemum*, in order that he might make his choice of these before the plants were lifted and divided. He sent a similar gift in 1825 and ten years later interpreted the 'something my wife calls everlastings' requested by Clare to mean chrysanthemums. By that date the poet was so ill that Henderson had to send these and other offshoots by the hand of a man who would plant them for him. His covering letter is the last in their correspondence.

OXEYE DAISY, *Leucanthemum vulgare*

Clare writes of this cheerful and conspicuous flower: 'The ox-eye is our "summer Daisy"; and, I believe, it is the only flower, almost, that the shepherd, ploughman, and milkmaid know by name, among the summer multitude' (Letters, 280). Another local name that he records is 'dog daisy' (NH, 17), and he appears to have learnt two more at Northampton. One occurs in "Twas in the midst of June...': ' the major meadow daisy's / Waved like the foaming surf' (LP, 718) and the other in 'My love she is a modest girl':

> In meadows and on meadow banks in baulks and clover too
> The white horse daisy's stand in ranks all silvered wi' the dew
>
> (LP, 723).

RAGWORTS and GROUNDSEL, *Senecio* spp.

Oxford Ragwort, *S. squalidus*, did not reach the East Midlands until the railway carried it there, so for Clare it is Common Ragwort, *S. jacobaea*, a 'humble flower with tattered leaves', that transforms the tawny autumn landscape:

> every where I walk
> Thy waste of shining blossoms richly shields
> The sun tanned sward in splendid hues that burn
> So bright and glaring that the very light
> Of the rich sunshine doth to paleness turn
> And seems but very shadows in thy sight
>
> ('The Ragwort', MP IV, 324).

Before long flocks of goldfinches would be feasting on the seeds of Common Ragwort (NH, 333), as they must have done earlier on the seeds of its sister species, Groundsel, *S. vulgaris* (NH, 44). This makes an appearance in *The Shepherd's Calendar* where, in the still air of a July heatwave, 'groundsels fairy downs / Unruffld keep their seeding crowns' (MP I, 94).

COLT'S-FOOT, *Tussilago farfara*

Clare must have known this early spring flower all his life, but in the great mass of his manuscripts it crops up only once, in a list of wild flowers jotted down eleven years after he entered the Northampton asylum (NH, 344).

POT MARIGOLD, *Calendula officinalis*

Clare grew marigolds in his own garden (NH, 214) and 'double marigolds' are named among garden pot herbs in 'The Cross Roads' (EP II, 628). The flowers could be used like saffron to colour dishes, but as its name implies, *C. officinalis* was chiefly valued for its medicinal properties. It is also, as gardeners well know, effective against blackfly, so, when the Village Doctress, in one of the additional stanzas of Clare's poem about her, tucks 'The mealy marigold of mellow hue' into her dress (MP III, 345), she may be using it less as an adornment than as an insect repellent.

SUNFLOWER, *Helianthus annuus*

Although this cottage-garden favourite makes only one appearance in Clare's poetry –

> sun flowers planting for their gilded show
> That scale the windows lattice ere they blow
> And sweet to 'habitants within the sheds
> Peep thro the diamond pane their golden heads
> > ('Rural Evening', EP II, 640)

– these lines, in which 'sheds' has its secondary meaning of 'poor dwellings', serve to suggest something distinctive about Clare's poetic vision. Nineteenth-century poetry abounds in heavily symbolic Sunflowers that turn towards the sun. Clare's in contrast turn towards their planter, as if to emphasise the intimacy between man and nature that underlies all his writing.

DAHLIAS, *Dahlia* cultivars

Although dahlias were not introduced to Europe from Central America until the last years of the eighteenth century, cultivars caught on rapidly in the gardens of England's great houses after the end of the Napoleonic wars. Several figure in lists that Clare made of plants that he had in all probability seen at Milton, while Henderson's letters reveal that he sent his friend young cuttings of *Dahlia* cultivars for both his Helpston and his Northborough garden.

Honeysuckle family, CAPRIFOLIACEAE

ELDERS, *Sambucus* spp.

The common Elder, *S. nigra*, which Clare usually spells 'eldern', makes an early appearance in his poetry: in 'The Wish' (EP I, 44), clumps of it are to be planted outside the dairy of his ideal house in order to keep the milk cool. But useful as the smell of its leaves might be in repelling flies, the straggly growth of Elder makes it a poor shade tree. The 'sickly elder' that loves 'To top the mouldering wall' in 'The Fate of Amy' (EP I, 271) and the 'one lonly eldern tree' that takes over the suicide's deserted garden in 'The Cross Roads' (EP II, 628) are more typical in that they are self-sown, or rather bird-sown. All the same, the Elder has its uses in Clare's world. Goldfinches nest in it ('Spring' ['The eldern opens…'], EP II, 582); the Village Doctress prepares an ointment from 'inner bark scraped from young eldern stalks' (MP III, 337); and, in what appears to be a communal activity, Helpston's 'industr[i]ous hus wives' make elderberry wine that the whole village drinks mulled at Christmas time ('October', MP I, 141).

One of these housewives was Clare's mother, who told him about a plant that was called 'Danewort' because it sprang up in places, including her native village, where Danish blood had been spilt in battle. She was speaking, mistakenly, of Greater Celandine; but Clare discovered from Elizabeth Kent's *Flora Domestica* that the name and the legend by right belonged to Dwarf Elder, *S. ebulus*, a perennial, non-woody species of elder (unrelated to that garden pest, Ground-elder, which belongs to the

Carrot family). What we do not know for sure is whether Clare had any first-hand knowledge of Dwarf Elder, which is rare around Helpston, though profuse and persistent in places where it does grow. This in itself suggests a plant that was introduced in the past for medicinal use, and there are twentieth-century records of *S. ebulus* being found beside the traces of the Roman road known as Ermine Street, and also quite close to Ann Clare's village of Castor, once a Roman settlement. So it may have arrived from the Continent long before any Danish invasion, and have acquired its name in Saxon times from its effect of inducing 'the danes' or diarrhoea. The association with Danish warriors would seem to be largely due to the Elizabethan historian, William Camden, who relates the legend in his *Britannia*. Still, it's a good story.

One small mystery is why Henderson wanted the Elder plants that he thanks Clare for in a letter of August 1828. If they were common Elder, he could presumably have found plenty for himself on the Milton estate. Can they have been the much rarer Dwarf Elder, or even the Guelder-rose of the next entry?

GUELDER-ROSE, *Viburnum opulus*

Chaucer, Proust and D. H. Lawrence are among the writers who have been captivated by this shrub's posy-like flower-heads, brilliant berries and richly coloured autumn foliage. But Clare, who knew it as 'water elder', as did Gertrude Jekyll, and recorded that it 'grows wild in our woods' (NH, 19), as it still does, gives it the barest of mentions in a late poem beginning 'The water elder is in flower' ('Summer', LP, 337).

HONEYSUCKLE or 'WOODBINE', *Lonicera periclymenum*

For Clare, 'woodbine' – he hardly ever calls it 'honeysuckle' – represents pure sensuous pleasure. He must often have caressed the downy undersides of its leaves, 'woodbines hairy sprout', as these 'earliest venturers to unfold their buds' emerged from dead-seeming stems ('March', MP I, 43; 'May-Noon', EP II, 388). Summer furnished a feast for the eye in creamy yellow flowers streaked with a pink that, in Clare's late love ditties, supplies a handy image for bright cheeks, just as the berries do for crimson lips. But when he speaks more personally in the poems he collected as *The Midsummer Cushion* he endows the flowers with a life of their own, recalling for example how, over the bubbling white sand of 'Round Oak Spring', 'the sweet woo[d]bine / Darkened and dipt its flowers' (MP IV, 280). 'Sweet', as always in Clare's writings, means scented, and in these poems the flowers' fragrance (strongest, he several times reminds us, after rain) joins in a synaesthetic blend with their appearance:

> And woodbines twisted fragrance there
> In many a yellow cluster shines
> > ('Walks in the Woods', MP III, 568).

A delicious flavour, too, was there for the biting: the late poem 'A Rhapsody' culminates in the taste of woodbine nectar 'seeth'd in the sunshine and the dew' (LP, 998). Only pleasures of the ear appear to be missing, and when Clare attempts a whole sonnet on the plant those too are supplied. While he is revelling in the scent of a hedge full of woodbine,

> some old ballad beautifully sung
> Comes through the hedge with crowded fragrance hung
> From merry maidens tossing up the hay
> > ('The Hedge Woodbine', MP IV, 350)

– a blend of pleasures that leaves him, poet though he is, with no words to express it.

Teasel family, DIPSACACEAE

WILD TEASEL, *Dipsacus fullonum*

This strikingly architectural plant was a familiar sight in Clare's countryside. One of his earliest poems vividly evokes the plant's 'jointed cup'– formed by the joining of paired leaves at each node of its main stalk – left dry and empty in the summer heat ('Noon' ['All how silent…'], EP I, 406).

In 'The Flitting' he recalls rabbit tracks on Helpston Heath that led 'Through beesom ling and teazle burrs' (MP III, 479) and in later years the sight of 'teazles prickly burrs' near the asylum brought back memories of his native village ('Recollections of Home', LP, 557).

FIELD SCABIOUS, *Knautia arvensis*

Commenting on the cultivated varieties of scabious described by Elizabeth Kent (whose book, anonymously published, he at first thought was the work of a man), Clare writes 'the common field Scabious is so beautiful that I wonder our tastful author did not put it in his garden' (NH, 21). No longer a cornfield weed, it still brings colour to road verges well into the autumn.

DEVIL'S-BIT SCABIOUS, *Succisa pratensis*

More accurately, 'bit by the Devil', whose resentment of its curative powers is one reason offered by folklore for this plant's stumpy rootstock. Clare writes of its 'dark purple flowers' (NH, 339) in the woodland rides of his home parish, where it can still be found in places where the soil is damp enough. Conservationists cherish it as the primary food-plant of the endangered Marsh Fritillary's caterpillar.

SWEET SCABIOUS, *Scabiosa atropurpurea*

One variety of this garden plant is so dramatically dark that Elizabeth Kent calls it 'almost black'. An early poem of Clare's, in which he describes it as 'jocolatley [i.e. chocolatley] dusk' ('The Wish', EP I, 47) shows that he had long wanted to possess it.

Ivy family, ARALIACEAE

IVIES, *Hedera* spp.

Ivy proliferates in Clare's early poetry, where it for the most part clothes ruins that have an air of being left over from the eighteenth-century craze for Gothic gloom. By the time of the *Midsummer Cushion* poems, such stagy settings have made way for a more rustic, Constable-style concept of the picturesque, so that Clare's account of 'Pleasant Places' begins with 'Old stone pits with veined ivy overhung' (MP IV, 224). He looks more directly at the plant in his prose writings, where he notes its springtime fruiting – 'The Ivy berrys too are quite ripe and the wood pigeons are busily fluskering among the Ivied dotterels' (i.e. old pollarded trees, NH, 60) – speculates on how injurious it is to its host ('I cannot deside against it', NH, 225), and recalls the custom of colouring its 'joccolate berrys' white or blue for a Christmas decoration (*By Himself*, 35).

All these references would have been to Common Ivy, *H. helix*, which is the ivy of eastern counties of England. But shortly after Clare moved to Northborough he asked the Vicar of Helpston to let him have cuttings of the 'Irish Ivy' (*Letters*, 591). Today we know this as the English name of a cultivar, *Hedera* 'Hibernica', which usually does not climb and is used as ground cover. This is a cultivar of Atlantic Ivy, *H. hibernica* – a native of the west of England (as well as Ireland) that is quite as rampant as *H. helix* and has the added advantage of larger, lighter-coloured and more spread-out leaves. In all probability Clare had admired a specimen in the Vicar's garden and envisaged it covering one of the walls of his starkly new house in the way that, according to a poem written a few years later, an ivy planted by himself had covered the gable end of his Helpston cottage. It is even possible that the ivy left behind at Helpston had been Irish Ivy; it must have been in some way distinctive for Clare to bring 'bits scarce a finger long' home from a ramble, and this accords with J. H. Chandler's records of specimens of this cultivar naturalised in the Soke (Wells, 2003). What is certain is that in 1837 Clare remembered with affection a plant whose life had long been entwined with his own:

> I often hear its rustle still
> And see its glossy leaves
> Peckt by the sparrows wanton bill
> On peaceful summer eve's

Tis music like a happy song
In healths delightful weather
Sung by a friend remembered long
When both were glad together

The quiet past there lives in bloom
Though time makes gaps between
And O may future joys to come
Be ivy ever green

('A long acquaintance...', MP V, 156).

Health's delightful weather changed all too quickly: four months after writing these lines Clare was prevailed upon to enter Matthew Allen's asylum.

Carrot family, APIACEAE

This family was once known as the Umbelliferae on account of the distinctive shape of its flower-heads, in which the stalks radiate from a central point to form a dome or a disk, either of which is very inviting to pollinators. Many of its genera have white or whitish flowers. At least four of these are alluded to by Clare, but he calls them by only two (appropriately) umbrella terms, 'kecks' (or 'kecksies') and 'hemlock', and even these appear to be interchangeable, at least in his pre-asylum poems. 'Hemlock' is still in use as a common English name, though it is now limited to a single species, *Conium maculatum*. The dialect word 'kecks' is a singular noun (the plural 'keckses' occurs in Shakespeare's *Henry V*), but Clare uses it both as a singular and a plural and applies it not only to living plants but also to the dry hollow stalks of large umbellifers – as when an old woman in 'The Summer Gone' (MP III, 490) gathers 'withered kecks' for fuel. Which plant is most likely to be meant by either 'kecks' or 'hemlock' in a particular context has to be deduced from the poem's indications of place and season.

156

COW PARSLEY, *Anthriscus sylvestris*

The Cow Parsley that foams gloriously along road verges every spring
needs both sunshine and shelter. Accordingly, in Clare's poetry we meet it
in open woodland as the 'crowding kecks' that conceal 'The Wood lark's
Nest' (MP IV, 322) and in a gap in an orchard as 'ramping kecks' that
'Shake like green neighbours in white caps' ('Evening', LP, 541). In other
poems, but at the same season and in the same type of habitat, it appears
under Clare's alternative name for an umbellifer:

> The hemlocks in the woodland hedge
> Are mounting to the awthorn bowers;
> Where white may comes a certain pledge
> With kingcups, and with daisey flowers
> > ('Spring' ['Tis glorious…'], LP, 338)

– while at the foot of a woodland maple,

> > the white hemlock with white umbel flowers
> Up each spread stoven to the branches towers
> And mossy round the stoven spread dark green
> And blotched leaved orchis and the blue bell flowers
> > ('The Maple Tree', LP, 1025).

FENNEL, *Foeniculum vulgare*

At the first sign that bees are preparing to swarm, the Village Doctress
hastens to attract them by rubbing down her new hives

> With balm and hairy fennel scented high
> That grows in monstrous bunches by the well

and then banging on her warming pan – 'As though they loved the sound',
Clare somewhat bemusedly adds (MP III, 339–40). What really lures them
is the fragrance of substances within the leaves that are identical with

those in the pheromone that is emitted by worker bees to attract their companions. 'Fennel's thread leaves' are put to the same use in the May section of *The Shepherd's Calendar* (MP I, 68). See also 'Balm' (p. 129).

HEMLOCK, *Conium maculatum*

In 'Cowper Green', 'hemlocks gloomy hue' (EP II, 182) must refer specifically to the purple-blotched stems that are a warning feature of the 'real', and highly poisonous, Hemlock, and because this early poem takes its title from a particular area of heathland, Druce was able to claim the allusion on Clare's behalf as a first record for Northamptonshire. *Conium maculatum*, however, is more at home near water – witness the dense three-metres-high stands of it beside fenland dykes – and when Clare writes, in a late poem with a river setting, 'Round hemlock flowers and kecksies fly's many a painted moth' ('Bonny Dark-eyed Susan', LP, 861), and in another,

> The hemlocks and keksies and Rue
> Grow rank by the side of the flood
>   ('What beauties the summer discloses…', LP, 1064),

he may again be distinguishing the poisonous Hemlock from umbellifers that he knew collectively as 'kecksies' or 'keksies'.

GARDEN PARSLEY, *Petroselinum crispum*

Before flat-leaved parsley became fashionable, the distinctive thing about Garden Parsley was its crimped foliage – 'Green curls the parsley rows in gardens trim' ('Fragment' ['The wind fanned daisys…'], LP, 901).

WILD ANGELICA, *Angelica sylvestris*

When blown through, the dry stalks of some umbellifers produce a most satisfying noise, as Clare records in 'The Last of Autumn': 'And keck made bugles spout their twanging sounds' (MP I, 343). In quoting this line Druce

158

recalls from his Northamptonshire childhood 'that whistles were made either of *Angelica* or *Heracleum Sphondylium* in S. Northants, the former for choice'. Was it the ridged stem that gave Wild Angelica the edge over Hogweed? Almost as tall as Hemlock, it grows like it by rivers, and is possibly paired with it in the two later poems referred to in the 'Hemlock' entry, above (p. 157), where 'kecksies' and 'hemlock' occur together. Druce claims 'kecks high flowers' from 'Rustic Fishing' (EP II, 643) as a first county record of Wild Angelica, but the reference is not precise enough to justify this; he also traces it wrongly to *The Shepherd's Calendar.*

HOGWEED, *Heracleum sphondylium*

Here is another vigorous and prolific white umbellifer, which in June takes over road verges from the spring-flowering Cow Parsley and which, to judge by its behaviour in the period of set-aside, must in Clare's day have run riot on fallow land. It is unlikely that he knew it as 'hogweed', which according to Anne Baker's *Glossary* was a Northamptonshire name for sowthistles; but under one or other of the umbrella terms 'kecks' and 'hemlock' he is likely to have gathered it as pig food and cut its dry stems to make whistles for his sons.

FLOWERING PLANTS – MONOCOTS

Sweet-flag family, ACORACEAE

SWEET-FLAG, *Acorus calamus*

Visiting 'Bates spinney' in March 1825, Clare came across 'a curious sort
of Iris or flag growing in a pond' (NH, 226). Grainger identified this as
Sweet-flag, a plant that has iris-like leaves with a spicy smell that caused it
to be introduced centuries earlier as a strewing herb. Its tiny flowers which,
like those of Lords-and-Ladies, grow on a fleshy axis (spadix), are very
different from those of the iris; but then it is unlikely that the tuber Clare
took home would ever have produced flowers, since Sweet-flag rarely does
this in Britain. Druce, who had known it since childhood, claimed to be
the first to record it in Northamptonshire, but Clare anticipates Druce's
record by some thirty-five years and also pinpoints a location, although he
does not clearly identify the plant. A rarity today, it has not been sighted in
the Soke for some years, although there are a few records of it growing in
the two bordering rivers, the Nene and the Welland.

Lords-and-Ladies family, ARACEAE

LORDS-AND-LADIES, *Arum maculatum* (plate 1)

Clare's own name for this was 'arum', but he introduced the name 'lords-
and-ladies' into several poems, knowing it would be more familiar to his
readers. The plant itself was a lifelong favourite: the leaves that figure
'glossy and rank' in one of his very last poems, written about 1860 ('Song
for Miss B—', LP, 1099), gave him as much pleasure as did the 'cone
curled leaves' (the flowered spathes), some of them 'stained wi spots of
jet', that he gathered as a child:

> How sweet it usd to be when april first
> Unclosd the arum leaves and into view

Its unlike spindle flowers their cases burst
Betingd wi yellowish white or lushy hue
      ('Impromptu at the Sight of Spring', EP II, 91).

The meaning of 'lushy' – not 'luxuriant', but 'deep-coloured' – is made plain in a later allusion to the spadices being 'Some the color o' cream others purple as blood' ('Bonny young Susan', LP, 942).

Duckweed family, LEMNACEAE

COMMON DUCKWEED, *Lemna minor*

'The old deep pond o' duckweed green' forms part of the setting for a moonlit tryst in one of Clare's late lyrics, 'I clasp my lovely girl' (LP, 804). A natural history note alludes to the plant less romantically, as 'duck meat' (NH, 106).

Water-plantain family, ALISMATACEAE

ARROWHEAD, *Sagittaria sagittifolia*

There is no mistaking the plant with leaves pointing out of the water like 'green shap'd arrow barbs' that Clare observes alongside other aquatics when taking 'A Walk in the Fields' (MP III, 384). But unless his term for it, 'frogwort', is an otherwise unrecorded local name for Arrowhead, he has misapplied a name that according to the *Essay on Weeds* of his contemporary Benjamin Holdich belonged to a species of orchid. Holdich was a local author, so Clare may have read the *Essay* on its publication in 1826, and this could explain his playing safe by not identifying 'the barbed leaf / Of waterweed bethread with lighter vein' in 'The Meadow Lake', written in 1832 (MP IV, 579). Eventually, though, he did learn the common name of this elegant plant, because a line in the late poem, ''Twas in a Summer's Morning', reads 'Through rustling flags and arrowhead The water wavered by' (LP, 777).

Flowering-rush family, BUTOMACEAE

FLOWERING-RUSH, *Butomus umbellatus* (plate 10)

In 'Gathering Wild Flowers' (MP II, 290), a boy sees 'the rush flower' in a pool, throws in a 'kickling' (wobbly) stone to stand on, falls off it, but holds on to his prize and decorates his hat with it. The beautiful pink umbel of lily-like flowers would have made a great cockade: any outrage felt by conservationist readers should be redirected at those who have destroyed the ponds and deep-channelled the rivers in which the Flowering-rush once flourished to a much greater extent than it does today.

Pondweed family, POTAMOGETONACEAE

PONDWEEDS, *Potamogeton* spp.

Three allusions to unspecified waterweeds in Clare's writings could all be to species of *Potamogeton*. In the asylum verses entitled 'Mary Helen from the Hill',

In the deep dyke grows the reed
The bullrush wabbles deeper still
And oval leaves of water weed
The dangerous deeper places fill   (LP, 1041).

Among *Potamogeton* species that have elliptical floating leaves, Broad-leaved Pondweed, *P. natans*, best fits the bill since it is to be found in still or slow-running water throughout Clare's countryside – shallow rather than deep water, but Clare may just be implying that it grows further in than do such marginal plants as club-rushes, then called 'bulrushes'. Maybe the talk of danger enables him to keep a tight hold of Mary Helen – which is as much as to say that we cannot take literally a late and not wholly coherent love-ditty.

Clare, however, is usually accurate in the descriptive poems he wrote in the mid 1820s. In one of these, 'A Walk in the Fields', he lists plants to be seen where a branch of the Welland widens out after flowing under Lolham Briggs. Among them, 'willow weed trailing wi long narrow leaves / The depth of the water full often deceives' (MP III, 384). There actually is a Willow-leaved Pondweed, *P.* × *salicifolius*, of which all the leaves, pointed at both ends like a willow's, are submerged. Druce, among others, records it for the Soke by its then name of *P.* × *decipiens*.

Both these quotations are from poems with a summer setting. A third allusion occurs in Clare's fifth Natural History Letter, written on 7 February 1825, in which he records among the other early signs of spring that 'water weeds with long silver green blades of grass are mantling the stagnant ponds in their summer liverys' (NH, 47). If this means an aquatic herb and a grass, their identities are anybody's guess (Grainger suggests one of the Water-starworts, *Callitriche* spp., and Reed Sweet-grass, *Glyceria maxima*). But if a single aquatic that forms a mat of grass-like leaves is meant, a submerged species of *Potamogeton* is a probability.

Black Bryony family, DIOSCOREACEAE

BLACK BRYONY, *Tamus communis*

Far apart in evolutionary terms, both Black Bryony and White Bryony are hedgerow climbers that have male flowers and female flowers followed by red berries on separate plants – a striking case of evolutionary convergence. Both are common in Clare's district, but he seems to have noticed the black more readily on account of its intensely shiny leaves which, he says, 'make up the want of flowers' ('Sunday Walks', EP II, 650 – the flowers are in fact there, but they are minute) and which, to paraphrase the second line below, cast distinctive shadows onto short grass:

In green like the ivy as dark and as rich
With a leaf twitting shades on the banks snubby sward
Just shapd like the hearts which we see on a card
('A Walk in the Fields', MP III, 389).

Herb-Paris family, MELANTHIACEAE

HERB-PARIS, *Paris quadrifolia* (plate 2)

'[F]ound for the first time "the herb true love" or "one berry" in Oxey Wood'. When Clare made this entry in his journal at the end of October 1824 (NH, 197), the Dog's Mercury that often conceals an isolated specimen of this 'cryptic and subtle woodland beauty' (as Richard Mabey calls it) would have died down, exposing the single black berry that remains after the fading of the four-fold structures that give the plant both its common and Latin names – paris meaning 'of equality'. Clare's own two names for it come straight out of Gerard's *Herbal*.

Lily family, LILIACEAE

The molecular system of classification has resulted in this family losing a large number of its genera to other families, especially to the Onion family, Alliaceae, and the Asparagus family, Asparagaceae (pp. 174–7).

FRITILLARY, *Fritillaria meleagris*

In his journal for 14 April 1825, Clare records that the 'Snake head or Frittellary' was in flower on that date (NH, 233–4). As he goes on to mention cultivated hyacinths, we may assume that his fritillaries were also garden-grown; there are no records of this beautiful chequered flower, Gerard Manley Hopkins's 'dapple-eared lily', ever having been found wild in the Helpston area.

Orchid family, ORCHIDACEAE

Among monocots, members of the Orchid family are as highly evolved as members of the Daisy family are among the dicots, and a number-count of known species shows them to be even more diversified; but in every other way the two families stand in striking contrast. Whereas the Asteraceae mass together their simple, single-seeded flowers with a view to attracting a range of pollinators, the Orchidaceae have evolved a huge range of highly complex flower forms, each of which is adapted to a very few pollinators – sometimes to a single species.

As more and more tropical orchids were discovered in the nineteenth century and methods of transporting and propagating them improved, orchid-collecting became a passion with the very rich – among them Charles Fitzwilliam, Lord Milton, whose head gardener, Joseph Henderson, was responsible for maintaining these exotics in the 'stove' at Milton Hall. Henderson's own interest, however, seems to have been in the wild orchids of the locality, such as Clare had for several years been collecting for his own garden. When Henderson and Clare became friends in 1822 they formed the perfect orchid-hunting partnership. Clare knew where to find the orchids and Henderson knew how to identify them. To aid Clare in his searches Henderson in the spring of 1828 copied out, mainly from Sir James Smith's text to Sowerby's *English Botany*, the descriptions of thirty 'English Orchises' (the form 'orchid' came in later), adding his own indications of which among them were already known to grow in Northamptonshire. Clare then wrote marginal notes in this guide, showing where he in turn had found thirteen of the species, and these notes are reproduced in Grainger's *Natural History Prose Writings of John Clare*, pp. 300–2. Many of the places named lie to the west and south-west of Helpston, in an area that Clare had begun to explore in the years before his marriage in company with another friend who was knowledgeable about orchids, Thomas Porter of Ashton.

Clare also made an orchid list – which Grainger reproduces – by using the inside cover of a gardening book published in 1819 to record all the wild orchids that he had transplanted to his garden (NH, 300). We do not know the dates of the entries in this list, nor how long individual plants survived, although in 1824 Clare claimed that the more common species had been thriving for many years (NH, 22). The secret of his success may be that he was careful to give them all plenty of their original soil, which would have contained the mycorrhizal fungi essential to their survival.

LADY'S-SLIPPER, *Cypripedium calceolus*

With its pouched yellow lip framed by long maroon wings, this is the most spectacular English orchid and the rarest. It was always limited to northern counties, where the depredations of plant hunters have resulted in its surviving into the present only as a single plant, along with some of its recent progeny, on a well-guarded site in Yorkshire. Sadly, we must count Joseph Henderson among the plunderers: in 1827 he gave Clare a plant of *C. calceolus* that he in all likelihood had obtained from his opposite number at the Fitzwilliam family's Yorkshire residence.

HELLEBORINES, *Epipactis* spp.

Among the 'Flowers promised me by Henderson' that Clare once jotted down (NH, 350–1) were a 'Ladys Slipper' and a 'Fen Orchis'. The latter was not the plant today known as Fen Orchid, *Liparis loeselii*, but Marsh Helleborine, *E. palustris*: Henderson used its Latin name when, in August 1827, he sent Clare a plant of it together with one of the Lady's-slipper (see the previous entry). Both were in all probability obtained from Yorkshire. But in Druce's time Marsh Helleborines, although very rare, could still be found in the Helpston area. He named Southorpe as one of the places where they grew; and in July 1830 Henderson had told Clare that he was 'very anxious to get to Southorpe heath before an orchis that grows there goes out of flower, it grows in a boggy place by the side of the brook'. So it is possible that he and Clare shared the delight of finding the subtly tinted whitish flowers of this July-flowering orchid.

Clare's collection (NH, 300) also included two 'Lily Leaved' orchids – a name used in gardening books of the time for Broad-leaved Helleborine, *E. helleborine*. Although this is the most widespread of the genus, having even colonised the green spaces of Glasgow, there are no recent records of it in Clare country.

COMMON TWAYBLADE and BIRD'S-NEST ORCHID, *Neottia* spp.

According to one of Clare's notes on Henderson's guide (NH 302), the Common Twayblade, *N. ovata*, formerly *Listera ovata* (plate 2), a tall yellow-green orchid that – as its names suggest – has two egg-shaped leaves, grew in a number of local woods, including Rice, or Royce, Wood close to Helpston village, the likeliest source of the two plants in his garden. The species is still to be found in the area.

The situation is otherwise with the strange-looking Bird's-nest Orchid, *N. nidus-avis*, which has no green leaves because it derives all its nutriment from a fungus. In May 1825 Clare had the good fortune to find what he described in his journal as 'a very scarce and curious orchis of an iron grey color or rather a pale rusty tinge with a root like the pile wort' (NH, 243). He added: 'I cannot make out its name', but sooner or later he must have done so because a 'Birds Nest' – so named on account of those thickened and entwined roots – occurs in the list of orchids he planted in his garden. Although the species has not been recorded in the Soke of Peterborough since the middle of the twentieth century, it may still linger there in the deep shade of ancient woodland.

GREATER BUTTERFLY-ORCHID, *Platanthera chlorantha*

The 'Butterflye' that occurs twice in Clare's orchid list owes its name to the appearance of its flowers; its pollinators are night-flying moths. In the margin of the guide made for him by Henderson he noted that it grew 'in Oxey-wood Open Copy Royce Woods and in most of the woods in this Neighbourhood rather plentifully' (NH, 300) – an impression that would have been helped by the way the long, shimmery-white flower-spikes show up in the half-light of woodland on a dull day. Today he would need to go a bit farther afield to find it; there are recent records from Castor Hanglands and Sutton Wood.

SMALL-WHITE ORCHID, *Pseudorchis albida*

When Henderson received a number of orchids from Clare in early July

1831, he wrote to say that 'the two small ones with whitish flowers I believe to be O[rchis] albida a species I have never found here'. Nowadays this orchid can only be found in the north and west of Britain, and Henderson may have discovered on closer inspection that what Clare had sent was a pale-flowered variety of a more common species. But Small-white Orchid had a much wider distribution in the nineteenth century, when it was even recorded in Kent and Sussex, so we cannot out of hand reject Henderson's suggestion, questionable though it is.

FRAGRANT-ORCHIDS, *Gymnadenia* spp.

Joseph Henderson, in his manuscript guide to English orchids, and Clare, in his marginal notes to the guide, both observe that the purplish-pink spikes of what they call the 'Aromatic orchis' are larger and taller when it grows in a moist place (NH, 300–2). But the difference was not in size alone. Genetic evidence has distinguished two distinct species: the Chalk Fragrant-orchid, *G. conopsea*, which thrives in what Henderson describes as 'old stone pits that have in the course of years become turfed over', and the Marsh Fragrant-orchid, *G. densiflora*, which is to be found in ground for which Clare uses the word 'moory', meaning marshy or boggy. Both have become very rare in the intensively farmed Soke. A tiny number of *G. densiflora* lingers on in a limestone flush not far from Helpston, and although *G. conopsea* appeared at one time to have found an ideal home in Barnack Hills and Holes, where it has been known to produce a thousand spikes in a season, that population is currently in decline.

Clare's marginal note on Henderson's 'Aromatic orchis' includes the dramatic statement that, while digging up plants of it near Ashton village, he 'found the broad lipped Military Orchis' (NH 301–2) – only one plant, he adds, so we must assume from 'Military' in his garden list that he uprooted it and took it home. But whatever he had found was not that Holy Grail of orchid-hunters, *Orchis militaris*. 'Broad-lipped Military Orchis' was the name then given by botanists to the Lady Orchid, *O. purpurea*. Less rare than *O. militaris*, this is nevertheless a very local species that has never been recorded north of the Thames valley. Admirers of Clare's plant-hunting skills may be tempted to recall that in the last century *O. militaris* established itself in Suffolk, and that the closely related Monkey Orchid, *O. simia*, appeared and flourished for a brief time on the Yorkshire coast. That said, probability is all against his claim to have found a Lady Orchid in the East Midlands.

FROG ORCHID, *Coeloglossum viride*

Henderson in his guide notes that 'This orchis is found sparingly among the old pastures in this neighbourhood'; but Clare found it 'in great plenty' in 'Herrings Park' (NH, 301) just south of the village of Ashton, home of his other orchid-fancying friend, Tom Porter. Today it continues to flower nearby, in Barnack Hills and Holes National Nature Reserve.

SPOTTED- and MARSH-ORCHIDS, *Dactylorhiza* spp.

The Common Spotted-orchid, *D. fuchsii*, grows in a range of habitats and consequently remains our most widespread orchid. It is the 'Pyramidial Spotted' of Clare's garden list; and in his comments on *Flora Domestica*, after describing the Early-purple and Green-winged Orchids, he writes: 'there is another sort later still that lifts on a tall stem a wreath of flowers in the form of a sugar loaf of a pale freckld colour' (NH, 16). It is of course the leaves that are spotted; the flowers' lips have delicate markings that recall Chinese calligraphy.

Before the Enclosures, when Clare was a boy guarding Helpston's cows as they grazed the low-lying 'moors' to the east and north of the village, handsome Early Marsh-orchids, *D. incarnata*, and probably Southern Marsh-orchids, *D. praetermissa*, as well (botanists had not yet distinguished the several species) were conspicuous in May and June; but by the time he wrote notes in Henderson's guide to orchids, these places were all ploughed up, and he had to search instead in 'closes' (meadows). It appears that he never got as far west across the Great North Road as the marshland known as White Water, where Druce and Charles Rothschild together found 'myriads of marsh orchids' early in the last century, but which is now a reservoir. But the good news is that determined searching is revealing new sites, the most recent for the Early Marsh-orchid being Castor Hanglands National Nature Reserves (2009), where it also crosses with the Common Spotted-orchid to give rise to the hybrid *D.* × *kernerorum*.

[TYPICAL] ORCHIDS, *Orchis* spp.

Elizabeth Kent's use, in her *Flora Domestica* (1823), of 'Cuckoo Flower' for *Cardamine pratensis* provokes Clare into insisting that this name belongs by right to Early-purple Orchid, *O. mascula* (plate 1):

> What the common people call 'cuckoo' with us is one which is a species of the 'Orchis' as Henderson tells me: there is a vast many varietys of them with us such as the 'bee Orchis' the 'pigeon Orchis' the 'flye Orchis' and 'butterfly Orchis' etc. etc. namd so from the supposd resemblance the flowers bear to those things these is my cuckoos and the one that is found in Spring with the blue bells is the 'pouch lipd cuckoo bud' I have so often mentioned its flowers are purple and freckld with paler spots inside and its leaves are spotted with jet... (NH, 15–16).

Abundant in woods in spring, Early-purple Orchids are no less abundant in Clare's poetry, from the 'gaping, speckled cuckoo-flowers' of his first collection ('Summer' ['The oak's slow-opening leaf...'], EP I, 521) to the 'cuckoo's / With freck'd lip, and hook'd nose' of a late 'Song' ('I pluck summer blossoms', LP, 270). He does not however use the colloquial 'cuckoo' in his natural history writing. So when in 1825 he found 'a large white Orchis in Oxey Wood of a curious species and very rare' (NH, 242) he in all probability consulted Henderson, who would have recognised it as a pure white specimen of *O. mascula*, known to him as the 'pigeon orchis' on account of its wing-like lateral sepals; and three days later Clare's journal records 'I found last week a fine white piegon Orchis which is seldom found' (NH, 243). The name surfaced in his mind many years later, when he included 'the pigeon winged orchis o' mulberry stain' in the flowery setting of 'Sweet Jenny Jones' (LP, 915).

Three orchid plants that were surviving in the shelter of Clare's privet hedge when he made his list appear in it as 'Green Man'. This was the name usually given at the time to Man Orchid, *O. anthropophora* (plate 13), in order to distinguish it from other species such as Military Orchid, *O. militaris*, which were commonly called 'man orchids'. Green certainly is the flower-spike's overall colour, though the lips of individual flowers, so strikingly like tiny human figures, can be mainly yellow or red. Away from its home territory in Kent the Man Orchid has always been very local, and it does not grow at all north of a line from Bristol to the Humber; when Henderson wanted to send plants of it to a friend in Yorkshire, Clare collected them for him – perhaps from old stone-pits on Helpston Heath, perhaps from Barnack Hills and Holes, where it has usually grown in profusion but has recently suffered a dramatic decline.

BURNT ORCHID, *Neotinea ustulata* (plate 5)

When Henderson was sent plants of this orchid by Clare, he identified them as the 'Dwarf Orchis', which was the usual name at the time for *N. ustulata*. But the deep reddish-brown purple of the unopened flowers makes Burnt, or Burnt-tip, Orchid a much better name. In the Soke it was sometimes called 'red-lead', after the pigment; and in his garden list Clare, who had long been familiar with it from the stone pits round Ashton, called it 'Red Man', an even more apt name, because the flower's lip is in the form of a sturdy little human figure under a 'hat' of petals and sepals that stay red-purple until the flower is fully open.

Burnt Orchid has now vanished from Clare country as from many other parts of Britain, where it is probably our fastest declining orchid.

PYRAMIDAL and GREEN-WINGED ORCHIDS, *Anacamptis* spp.

'Pyramidial Plain' is Clare's name in his garden list for the richly pink *A. pyramidalis* of late summer to which we still give the centuries-old name of the Pyramidal Orchid, although the spikes often lose their pointed shape when they are fully open. Clare's notes of where it was to be found (NH, 300–1) suggest that in his time it was, as Henderson's guide states, 'not uncommon'. Nowadays it is rare in the Soke with the exception of Barnack Hills and Holes, where it is present in quantity.

The Green-winged Orchid, *A. morio*, formerly *Orchis morio* (plate 5), was for Clare the cuckoo-flower that 'comes on the pastures a little later then the wood sort [i.e. the Early-purple Orchid] and blossoms in a variety of colours such as pink lilac and dark purple' (NH, 16). Many years later he was still pairing the two species in verse –

> Bluebells and cuckoo's in the wood
> And pasture cuckoo's too   ('Wild Flowers', LP, 362).

It was a pairing that went back to the medieval herbalists, who gave gender to many species. The tradition lingered in gardening books such as John Abercrombie's *Practical Gardener* (owned by Clare), where *Orchis mascula* is 'Male' and *Anacamptis morio* 'Female or Meadow', and Clare follows it in his garden list, where number 11 is 'Female or Meadow' and number 13 'Male or Wood' (NH, 300).

Woods round Helpston still provide a home for Early-purple Orchids, but the 'improvement' of grassland has led to the exquisite Green-winged Orchid's mainly surviving in nature reserves.

FLY, EARLY SPIDER- and BEE ORCHIDS, *Ophrys* spp.

While orchids such as the Military Orchid owe their names to human fancifulness, there is a real affinity between species of *Ophrys* and the insects after which botanists have named them: the resemblance of their flowers to the specific form of certain female insects tricks the relevant males into an attempt at copulation, in the course of which pollination may occur. This startling fact was not known until the twentieth century, but the genus has always held a special fascination for naturalists, John Clare and Joseph Henderson among them.

'[W]here the Divel did you find the fly Orchis'? Henderson demanded to know when, in 1827, Clare first sent him plants of *Ophrys insectifera* (plate 3). The answer was not 'at the north end of Hilly Wood', as Clare's marginal note to Henderson's 'paper on the Orchises' (NH, 302) would lead us to expect, but 'in Oxey Wood', because in February 1830 Henderson asked him to get two or three more plants from there, the ones sent in 1827 having died. Evidently he relied on Clare being able to detect, amid the old year's leaf litter, the leaves of this wintergreen species. It is not pollinated by flies, but by a species of digger wasp which survives in the area, though the orchids have long since disappeared.

Both Early Spider-orchid, *O. sphegodes*, and Bee Orchid, *O. apifera* (plate 6), were to be found in Clare's time on the grassed-over declivities of old quarries such as the one Clare knew as 'Swordy Well': the name furnishes the title of a sonnet in which the poet speaks of

> Haunting thy mossy steeps to botanize
> And hunt the orchis tribes where natures skill
> Doth like my thoughts run into phantasys
> Spider and Bee all mimicking at will   (MP IV, 145).

Other stone-pits where both species flourished lay close to the hamlet of Ashton and to the villages of Barnack and Ufford. Both also grew, Clare tells us, in the park of Walcot House, just to the south of Barnack, and farther south again on Southorpe Heath; but in spite of their having shared many sites in the past, the two species have had very different fates.

Early Spider-orchids – which in fact mimic, not a spider, but the burly form of a solitary bee – have always been harder to find than Bee Orchids. Clare and Henderson knew several sites in the Soke, but so too did several leading nineteenth-century botanists and their over-collecting, however 'scientific', must have contributed to a decline that was completed by the twentieth-century destruction of habitat. There are no Early Spider-orchids now in Clare country.

The Bee Orchid fared better, which may have something to do with the fact that it does not, in Britain at least, rely on pollination by bees but is self-fertilising. Not only has it held its own in the Soke, but it is slowly spreading there. One place where its reappearance is specially welcome is the Swaddywell Pit nature reserve, which is situated to the east of the site of Clare's Swordy Well. Here, careful management of the landfill covering a deep quarry of the 1920s (as distinct from the reserve's present-day 'pit', which is a relic of 1960s quarrying) has had the effect of at long last restoring Bee Orchids to Helpston Heath.

Iris family, IRIDACEAE

YELLOW IRIS, *Iris pseudacorus* (plate 8)

'[Y]ellow flag flowers rustling in the dyke' ('Summer Evening', EP II, 389) were very much a feature of the wetlands that Clare knew; fine enough to be garden flowers, he says in 'The Meadow Grass' (MP III, 558), where they rather unconvincingly 'tower' in imitation of the irises of another botanically-minded poet, Charlotte Smith (see NH, 20). In the asylum poems their name changes to the Scots 'water skeggs' ('The Willow shaded Lane', LP, 585; 'Fair Maria, LP, 721). Had Clare picked up this name in his rambles with Joseph Henderson, a Scot?

SPRING CROCUS, *Crocus vernus*

Clare's pleasure in crocuses as the forerunners of spring best shows itself at the end of his long account of a waterlogged winter at Northborough–

> Such is our lowland scenes that winter gives
> And strangers wonder where our comfort lives
> Yet in a little garden close at home
> I watch for spring and there the crocus comes
>   ('Now winter in his earnest mood...', MP V, 175).

Asphodel family, XANTHORRHOEACEAE

ALOE, *Aloe* sp.

In one of Clare's late love lyrics, 'My bonny Jane', bees in a cottage garden 'searched the alloes bloom' (LP, 747). Spectacular as this plant's flower-spike would have appeared in such a setting, the growers would most have valued it for the supposed curative powers of the drug 'aloes' (not a plural) that could be extracted from the huge spiny leaves. All known species originated in Africa, but in Clare's time the 'true' Aloe, *Aloe vera*, that is held in such high esteem in alternative medicine was grown in Barbados for the European market.

Onion family, ALLIACEAE

ONION and LEEK, *Allium* spp.

Two humble but valued members of the Onion family, the Onion, *A. cepa*, and the Leek, *A. porrum*, gain a mention in a late fragment of verse ('The wind fanned daisies…'), which includes the sowing of both among the signs that spring is on its way (LP, 901). We also learn from 'St Martin's Eve' that on the evening of 10 November girls would sleep with a red onion under their pillow in order to dream of a future husband (MP III, 275).

JERSEY LILY or 'NAKED LADY', *Amaryllis belladonna*

When, in July 1833, Henderson sent Clare an assortment of plants to brighten his Northborough garden, he was careful to include late-blooming species such as this starkly leafless pink lily, which had been introduced from the Cape of Good Hope in the eighteenth century. Realising, perhaps, that his severely depressed friend might lack the willpower to lift and store bulbs, he suggested 'a little half rotten dung' as a means of helping *Amaryllis* to survive the fenland winter.

SPRING SNOWFLAKE, *Leucojum vernum*

The recipient of 'Song to J…– W…–' excels, in her beauty, 'The snow-flake fair o' ember week' (LP, 659) – the ember days of early Lent being just the time in the Church's calendar when *Leucojums*, as they are often called today, are likely to be in flower in gardens.

SNOWDROP, *Galanthus nivalis*

Widely naturalised though it has become, the Snowdrop is an introduced species. It can flower in gardens as early as late January, so it is not surprising that it figures in a number of the valentines that Clare, in his asylum years, wrote for lovers to offer their sweethearts on St Valentine's Day, 14 February.

DAFFODIL, *Narcissus pseudonarcissus*

There are no records of the native wild Daffodil growing in the vicinity of Helpston, and Clare would have grown up thinking of daffodils as garden flowers:

> Warm daffodils about the garden beds
> Peep through their pale slim leaves their golden heads.
> ('Home Pictures in May', MP IV, 261).

However, the very first poem transcribed for him by the house-steward of the Northampton asylum, a flower-strewn love lyric dated May 1844, declares that

> The rich valley lillies
> The wood daffodillies
> Have been found in our rambles when Summer began
> ('Song' ['I pluck Summer blossoms...'] LP, 270).

It is just possible that here Clare is recording a recent discovery of his own, but although wild Daffodils could and can still be found in central Northamptonshire, they are limited to ancient woodland. To me the poem – dashed off, a bit erotic, and with a fine mix of spring and summer flowers – reads as a recall of the months in 1818 when he was courting Patty near Casterton in Rutland. 'Rich valley lilies' such as he then picked for her (see the next entry) have gone for good, but 'wood daffodillies' can be found not far away. As with the 'daffies' of another asylum poem ('Mary a Ballad', LP, 514) Clare calls them by a village variant on their name.

Asparagus family, ASPARAGACEAE

LILY-OF-THE-VALLEY, *Convallaria majalis*

In the summer of 1818 Clare was working at Casterton, about ten miles from Helpston, and courting a local girl, Martha Turner, who would shortly become his wife Patty. One of his fragments of an autobiography records their wandering 'in more then happiness' in a wood 'coverd with Lilys of the valley of which she usd to gather handfulls for her flower pots and I helpd her to gather them' (*By Himself*, 92) – an experience that inspired lines of *The Shepherd's Calendar*:

> And stooping lilys of the valley
> That comes wi shades and dews to dally
> White beading drops on slender threads
> Wi broad hood leaves above their heads
> Like white robd maids in summer hours
> Neath umberellas shunning showers   ('May', MP I, 63).

BLUEBELL, *Hyacinthoides non-scripta* (plate 1)

When Clare's first collection of poems appeared in 1820 Bluebells were still generally known as 'harebells', although the name now so familiar to us for the plant that has been voted the English national flower was already coming into use. In 'The Nightingale's Nest', written in 1832 (MP III, 460, 456), the beauty of the bird's song is linked to the beauty of the 'harebells' round its nest. But a child who is also in the wood is gathering 'blue bell flowers' and this suggests that the name was changing with a new generation. By the time Clare was moved to the Northampton asylum, he had finally settled on 'bluebells' as the name of the flowers with 'crispy curls' and 'sapphire stems' that he recalled in 'O for one real imaginary blessing' (LP, 224) and other late poems.

TASSEL HYACINTH, *Muscari comosum*

When Clare celebrated his thirty-second birthday in the Steward's Room at Milton Hall, Joseph Henderson promised to give him a 'Feather Hyacinth' among other plants (NH, 250). This very pretty grape-hyacinth was brought to Britain as long ago as the sixteenth century. In some south-western areas it has even naturalised and been demoted to the status of 'persistent weed'.

Bulrush family, TYPHACEAE

BRANCHED BUR-REED, *Sparganium erectum*

In 'The Wild-flower Nosegay', Clare tells us that as a child he spent hours looking for 'prickly burs that crowd the leaves of sedge' (EP II, 411). He would have had to look in dykes and ditches and in branches of the Welland, though this striking plant (not a sedge), with its round clusters of flowers along each stem – male above, female below – and its shining dark fruit beloved of wildfowl, has never been hard to find in the district. It must also have grown in the Nene at Northampton, because the sight there of 'little hubs of sedge' brought back to Clare memories of the countryside in which he had grown up ('Recollections of Home', LP, 557).

BULRUSH, *Typha latifolia*

The black poker-like flower-heads of this aquatic plant are so common – and so attractive – that it comes as a surprise to find that Clare has only one allusion to them, as distinct from several mentions of Common Club-rush by its then prevalent name of 'bulrush'. In one of his Northborough sonnets, a cowherd wades into a dyke to gather 'fox tail flags that grow above the brig / And burrs more green and only half as big' ('The old dyke full…', MP V, 371). Strikingly taller than the 'burrs' (bur-reeds: see previous entry), the 'fox tail flags' are almost certainly the plants we now know as Bulrushes.

Rush family, JUNCACEAE

RUSHES, *Juncus* spp.
WOOD-RUSHES, *Luzula* spp.

Rushes abound in Clare's poetry as they did in his landscape. The most common, then as now, was Hard Rush, *J. inflexus*: Druce believed it to be the species that the poet had in mind in the much-loved lyric that begins 'Swamps of wild rush beds' ('Song', EP II, 100). The rushes that Clare as a child plaited into whips and 'a rural crown' ('Summer Morning', EP I, 554; 'Childish Recollections', EP II, 300) are likely to have been Soft-rush, *J. effusus*, rather than (pace Druce) the similar but less common Compact Rush, *J. conglomeratus* – unless, that is, they were Common Club-rush, which is in fact a sedge: see the next entry.

In two of his asylum poems Clare alludes to a 'tasselled' rush. The adjective could just be generally descriptive, but if he was using it to distinguish a particular kind of rush he may have in mind the loose flower-heads of some wood-rushes, of the genus *Luzula*. In the rather confused 'I love the blue violet' (LP, 814), the presence of anthills suggests a grassland setting such as Field Wood-rush, *L. campestris*, is at home in; and in fact 'the wind waving rush' here spoken of has already appeared in the same kind of habitat in an earlier poem:

> Wind waving rush left to bewildered ways
> Shunning the scene which cultures toil devours
> > ('Forest Flowers', MP IV, 274).

But in the other late poem, 'The Sailor's Return',

> The rush nods and bows till its tassel'd head tipples
> Right into the whimpled flood kissing the stones   (LP, 955)

and here, unless Clare is loosely using 'rush' for 'reed', we appear to have come across a tasselled rush with a liking for streamsides, namely Great Wood-rush, *L. sylvatica*, which has become rare in the Soke.

Sedge family, CYPERACEAE

COMMON CLUB-RUSH, *Schoenoplectus lacustris*

In the July section of *The Shepherd's Calendar* (MP I, 90), an enterprising gipsy ties a reaping hook to a pole in order to cut club-rushes – which Clare knew as 'bulrushes' – and hawk them round the district as material for re-seating chairs; the unjointed stems, up to three metres long, were ideal for the job. Clare's allusions show that he was fascinated by their pliability; he has recourse to the language of Psalm 107 (in the Book of Common Prayer version) to describe how, in running water, they 'reeled and staggered / Like any drunken man' ('Rhymes In the Meadows', MP III, 577).

SEDGES, *Carex* spp.

Mixed with horsetails and rushes round a pond's edge in 'Wanderings in June' are razor-sharp 'cutting leaves of sedge / That children learn to dread' (MP I, 313). Druce identified this as Greater Pond-sedge, *C. riparia*, which is tall enough to produce the 'brustling' or 'sighing' that Clare alludes to in several poems (e.g. 'The Woodman' ['Now evening comes…'], MP IV, 212). Sedges of one species or another, among the eight or nine still readily to be found in Clare's district, provide moorhens with nesting material ('The Last of March', EP II, 474) and are the haunt of their own special bird, the sedge-warbler: see 'The Sedge Bird's Nest' (MP IV, 153). The sedge that in 'Noon' is 'Ramping in the woodland hedge' (EP I, 405) is probably Wood-sedge, *C. sylvatica* (rather than Pendulous Sedge, *C. pendula*, which is less frequently seen in Clare's part of the Soke) and this could also be the one used by the shepherd boy in *The Shepherd's Calendar* to cover his rough shelter of wattles ('March', MP I, 41–2).

Grass family, POACEAE

The importance of this family, formerly known as Gramineae, comes home to us when we reflect that grasses, whether they occur in wild

communities or as planted crops, are reckoned to make up four-fifths of
the English landscape. Wading through tall grasses is many people's earliest
and profoundly sensuous experience of the plant world. Clare recaptures
its pleasures in 'The Meadow Grass',

> Pit patting at ones legs to feel
> Their seeded heads then bounce away (MP III, 556).

and the best-known of all his poems ends with the longing to

> sleep as I in childhood, sweetly slept,
> Untroubling, and untroubled where I lie,
> The grass below – above the vaulted sky.
>> ('I Am', LP, 397)

PERENNIAL RYE-GRASS, *Lolium perenne*

The girl who, in one of Clare's late poems, 'plucked a bent… / And bowed
her head to count the seeds' was in all probability playing 'loves-me-loves-
me-not' by pulling off the alternating florets on a spikelet of Perennial
Rye-grass ('Song' ['The hay was mown…'], LP, 608). See below under
'Bents' (p. 182) for this generalised use of the name.

QUAKING-GRASS, *Briza media*

Clare's children picked this very pretty grass, which has heart-shaped
spikelets trembling on the thinnest of stems, when the family strolled
through pastures on their 'Sunday Walks' (EP II, 648). They knew it as
'totter grass', as did their father, for whom one of the greatest 'Pleasures of
Spring' was cloud-gazing when 'Stretched mid the totter grass and nodding
flowers' (MP III, 54). Sad to tell, Quaking-grass is far less common now
that there are hardly any unimproved pastures round Helpston. It can still
be found, however, in Torpel Manor Field, across which Clare would have
walked to Ashton and Barnack.

OAT, *Avena sativa*

In May, according to *The Shepherd's Calendar*, village girls weave love-knots from either 'blue green oat or wheaten blade' (MP I, 65: see under 'Reed Sweet-grass' below, p. 184). But by August each grain crop has ripened to its distinctive colour:

> The wheat tans brown and barley bleaches grey
> In yellow garb the oat land intervenes (MP I, 118).

Oats were grown chiefly as horse fodder and, since horses were the chief means of transport at the time, the nation's oat crop was as vital to it then as its supply of diesel and petrol is today.

TUFTED HAIR-GRASS, *Deschampsia cespitosa*

As he takes us in search of 'The Nightingale's Nest', Clare tells us to

> part aside
> These hazel branches in a gentle way
> And stoop right cautious neath the rustling boughs
> For we will have another search today
> And hunt this fern strown thorn clump round and round
> And where this seeded woodgrass idly bows
> We'll wade right through it is a likely nook
> In such like spots and often on the ground
> They'll build where rude boys never think to look
> Aye as I live her secret nest is here
> Upon this white thorn stulp...   (MP III, 458–9).

'Woodgrass' in this passage is identified by Druce as Tufted Hair-grass, *Deschampsia cespitosa*. This is a tall, tussocky grass which Clare names as a refuge of hares in 'The Summer Gone' (MP III, 490) and 'Wood Pictures in Winter' (MP IV, 240). Its flowers can be silvery in colour, and this, or perhaps the bleached appearance of its dead leaves, could account for the variant 'And where the seeded grass hangs long and grey' in the poem as it was printed in the gift album *Friendship's Offering* (1833).

YORKSHIRE-FOG, *Holcus lanatus*

Clare once nearly stepped on a snipe that was, he thought, 'preparing a nest in the midst of a large tuft of fog or dead grass common on the heaths' (NH, 155). 'Fog' is from a Norse word for hayfield grass left standing in winter; by a happy chance it brings to mind the pink-purple mist that Yorkshire-fog in flower spreads over a meadow.

REED CANARY-GRASS, *Phalaris arundinacea*

We think of ornamental grasses as a very modern garden fashion, but a striped variety of the native Reed Canary-grass, known to Clare as 'lady's laces', had by his time been grown for centuries in cottage gardens such as the one in 'The Cross Roads' (EP II, 628). (Anne Baker's identification of it as *Calamagrostis*, or Small-reed, is almost certainly mistaken.)

BENTS, *Agrostis* spp.

In the long title poem of *The Village Minstrel*, Clare's invocation of his Rural Muse begins

> Simple enchantress, wreathd in summer blooms
> Of slender bent stalks topt wi' feathery down   (EP II, 435).

By Clare's time botanists had settled on 'bent' as the English name for the grass genus *Agrostis*, and Druce plumped for Common Bent, *A. capillaris*, as the plant meant here and in many other passages. However, I think Clare was more familiar with Creeping Bent, *A. stolonifera*, another slender (and rather more feathery) grass, which is much more plentiful in his district. But the question becomes, as they say, academic when we realise that 'bent' traditionally was used for any wiry-stemmed grass: see the entry above

(p. 180) for 'Perennial Rye-grass'.

TIMOTHY, *Phleum pratense*

Timothy Hanson, whose introduction of this nutritious meadow grass to America is commemorated in its name, was unknown to Clare, who uses a version of the older common name of 'cat's-tail grass' when, for example, he is writing about an evening walk through the countryside:

> How beautiful it is to leave
> The paths o' sultry day
> At dewy fall o' quiet Eve
> Through coppices to stray
> Where cat-tail grass nodds o'er the path
> And rabbits come to feed...
>
> ('How beautiful it is', LP, 711).

REED SWEET-GRASS, *Glyceria maxima*

In June 1846 Clare wrote 'The Round Oak', which begins:

> The Apple top't oak in the old narrow lane
> And the hedge row of bramble and thorn
> Will ne'er throw their green on my visions again
> As they did on that sweet dewy morn
> When I went for spring pooteys and birds nests to look
> Down the border of bushes ayont the fair spring
> I gathered the palm grass close to the brook
> And heard the sweet birds in thorn bushes sing   (LP, 450).

The spot remembered here was already the subject of half a dozen poems, beginning in 1818 with the powerful 'Lamentations of Round Oak Waters' – all of them protesting at the Enclosers' spoliation of a particularly beautiful stream that rose from a spring to the south-west of Helpston. But after nearly seven years in the Northamptonshire asylum, Clare appears to have forgotten the unwelcome changes wrought by the Enclosures and to feel only the pain of his enforced separation from the scenes of his childhood:

> Thy limpid brook flows and thy waters rejoice
> And I long for that tree – but my wishes are vain   (LP, 451).

'Palm grass' is almost certainly Reed Sweet-grass, which grows in or by water throughout Clare's district. It has handsome feathery flower-heads somewhat like those of Common Reed, *Phragmites australis*, but its leaves are less coarse and more strap-shaped and so are likely to have been the 'broad green reed blades' with which, in 'The Rivals' (MP I, 215), two village youths make 'love knott platts'. Anne Baker, in the glossary of Northamptonshire words that she wrote with Clare's help, defined such plaits as 'spells or charms, made by rustics, of the blades of the oat or wheat, and sometimes of the reed-blade'. The spell, or rather divination, appears to have consisted of intertwining two blades of whichever grass was being used by folding them one over the other at right angles; if the blades stayed together the maker's love was reciprocated, but if they sprang apart he or she longed in vain.

'Palm' in this Northamptonshire name suggests that Reed Sweet-grass leaves were also used to make the crosses given out at church on Palm Sunday.

COMMON COUCH, *Elytrigia repens*

'Twitch' is Clare's name for this aggressive weed. Its deep and tough roots foul ploughshares, so that ploughmen

> often stop their songs to clean their ploughs
> From teasing twitch that in the spongy soil
> Clings round the colter   ('March', MP I, 40).

knowing that, if allowed to grow, 'the matted twitches run' with a vigour that excludes light from the growing crop ('Solitude', EP II, 340). The only way to deal with this pest in Clare's day was to dig it up and burn it. Smoke rising 'from the twitch heap among the green corn' ('The Wind', LP, 615) was as much a feature of his landscape as was 'thin smoke without flame / From the heaps of couch-grass' in Thomas Hardy's.

SIX-ROWED BARLEY, *Hordeum vulgare*

In traditional English agriculture barley was second only to wheat in importance, and barley fields are very much part of Clare's poetic landscape. A great deal of the crop was destined for the brewhouse; but 'barley crust', rather than wheaten bread, is also the cottager's staple fare in Clare's poems. In 'The Village Minstrel' he writes, with his incapacitated father in mind, of an old age so enfeebled that 'labour scarce its barley crust supplies' (EP II, 137). In better times, however, the lightness of his mother's barley dumplings was something to boast about ('To Captain Sherwill Jun.', EP II, 66).

BREAD WHEAT, *Triticum aestivum*

The source of daily bread to those who could afford it, wheat was to the inhabitants of Clare's village their most vital crop and the most demanding of labour. We are kept aware of those demands throughout *The Shepherd's Calendar*, right up to the time that the first hard frosts put an end to ploughing. Even then the thresher's toil continued, and as a child Clare helped his father to thresh. Children also worked hard in the wheatfields, weeding, bird-scaring and, at harvest-time, gleaning. The picturesque account of gleaning in 'Valentine Eve', where the reaper, a disguised aristocrat in love with the gleaner,

> oft would stop to wet his hook and smile   *whet*
> And loose when none percieved from out his hand
> Some wheat ears now and then upon the land   (MP III, 74)

is less convincing than the misery of the hot, tired child, his bare feet cut by stubble, who gleans alongside his mother in 'August' (MP I, 119).

As a result, perhaps, of these childhood experiences, Clare tends to see a field of wheat from a near-ground level at which it is a less than safe refuge for many forms of life: colourful flowers that have to be weeded out in May; nesting birds such as larks, quails, partridges and the elusive 'landrail' (corncrake); harvest mice; even the odd courting couple. At this level, the wheat spear itself is close enough to the eye to be seen in fine detail as it breaks into flower

> And splits the bondage of its case in two
> And bunches more forward een then others towers
> Quite out – soon hung with dusty threads of flowers
> ('The summer was delicious ...', MP V, 20).

COMMON REED, *Phragmites australis*

Although some of the reeds in Clare's descriptions of rivers and wetlands may have been Reed Sweet-grass (see p. 184 above), others, such as the 'black-topt reeds / In little forrests' that he observes on 'A Walk' (MP IV, 312) and those that he likens to ostrich feathers in 'A Walk in the Fields' (MP III, 384), must have been the Common Reed that grows profusely north and east of Helpston, in dykes and in the slow-flowing branches of the Welland.

Principal Sources

Abercrombie, John, *Abercrombie's Practical Gardener*, second edition (London, 1817)

Abercrombie, John, *The Gardener's Companion* (London, 1822)

Bailey, Brian J., 'Clare's ruined village: Pickworth, Leicestershire', *Country Life*, 116 (21 April 1977), 996

Baker, Anne Elizabeth, *Glossary of Northamptonshire Words and Phrases* (London, 1854), two volumes

Baker, George, *History of Northamptonshire* (London, 1822–41), two volumes

Bate, Jonathan, *John Clare: A Biography* (London: Picador, 2003)

Berkeley, Miles, [Obituary of Joseph Henderson], *Proceedings of the Linnean Society*, 25 (1866–7), 35

Berkeley, Miles, [Obituary of Joseph Henderson], *Gardeners' Chronicle and Agricultural Gazette*, 48 (1866), 1138

Barrell, John, *The Idea of Landscape and the Sense of Place 1730–1840: an Approach to the Poetry of John Clare* (London: Cambridge University Press, 1972)

Bricknell, Christopher, ed., *The Royal Horticultural Society, Gardeners' Encyclopedia of Plants and Flowers* (London: Dorling Kindersley, 1994)

Britten, James, and Holland, Robert, *A Dictionary of English Plant Names* (London, 1886)

Campbell-Culver, Maggie, *The Origin of Plants: The People and Plants that have shaped Britain's Garden History since the Year 1000* (London: Headline, 2001)

Cherry, J. L., *Life and Remains of John Clare* (London and Northampton, 1873)

Chilcott, Tim, *A Publisher and his Circle: The Life and Work of John Taylor* (London: Routledge and Kegan Paul, 1972)

Clapham, A. R., Tutin, T. G. and Moore, D. M., *Flora of the British Isles*, third edition (Cambridge: Cambridge University Press, 1987)

Clare, John, *Poems Descriptive of Rural Life and Scenery* (London: Taylor and Hessey; Stamford, E. Drury, 1820)

— *The Village Minstrel and Other Poems* (London: Taylor and Hessey; Stamford, E. Drury, 1821), two volumes

— *The Shepherd's Calendar; with Village Stories, and Other Poems* (London: Taylor and Hessey; Stamford, E. Drury, 1827)

— *The Rural Muse: Poems* (London: Whittaker, 1835)

— *The Natural History Prose Writings of John Clare*, ed. Margaret Grainger (Oxford: Clarendon Press, 1983)

— *The Later Poems of John Clare 1837–1864*, ed. Eric Robinson and David Powell, assoc. ed. Margaret Grainger (Oxford: Clarendon Press, 1984), two volumes, pagination throughout

— *The Letters of John Clare*, ed. Mark Storey (Oxford: Clarendon Press, 1985)

— *The Early Poems of John Clare 1804–1822*, ed. Eric Robinson and David Powell, assoc. ed. Margaret Grainger (Oxford: Clarendon Press, 1989), two volumes

— *John Clare: By Himself*, ed. Eric Robinson and David Powell (Ashington and Manchester: Mid-Northumberland Arts Group and Carcanet, 1996)

— *Poems of the Middle Period 1822–1837*, ed. Eric Robinson, David Powell and P. M. S. Dawson (Oxford: Clarendon Press, Vols I–II, 1996, Vols III–IV, 1998, Vol. V, 2003), five volumes in all

[Clare, John, as recipient] 'Original Letters addressed to John Clare, the Peasant Poet', Egerton MSS, British Museum MS 2,249–55

Clarke, W. A., *First Records of British Flowering Plants* (London, 1897)

Culpeper, Nicholas, *The English Physician and Complete Herbal* (London, 1789 and 1792 editions)

Dean, E. Barbara, 'John Clare at Lolham Bridges', *John Clare Society Journal*, 2 (1983), 24–7

De Wilde, G. J., Rambles *Roundabout and Poems* (Northampton, 1872)

Druce, George Claridge, *The Flora of Northamptonshire* (Arbroath: T. Buncle, 1930)

Emmerton, Isaac, *A Plain and Practical Treatise on the Culture and Management of the Auricula, Polyanthus, Carnation, Pink, and the Ranunculus* (London, 1819)

Foss, Arthur, and Trick, Kerith, *St Andrew's Hospital, Northampton: The First*

150 Years, 1838–1988 (Cambridge: Granta Editions, 1989)

Gaull, Marilyn, 'Clare and "the dark system"' in *John Clare in Context*, ed. Hugh Haughton, Adam Phillips and Geoffrey Summerfield (Cambridge: Cambridge University Press, 1994), 279–94

Gent, Gill, and Wilson, Rob, *et al.*, *The Flora of Northamptonshire and the Soke of Peterborough* (Rothwell: Robert Wilson Designs, 1995)

Gent, Gill, and Wilson, Rob, *The Flora of Northamptonshire and the Soke of Peterborough* (Rothwell: Robert Wilson Designs, 2012)

Gerard, John, *The Herball or Generall Historie of Plantes … Enlarged and amended by Thomas Johnson* (London, 1633)

Gerard, John, *A Catalogue of Plants Cultivated in the Garden of John Gerard*, ed. B. D. Jackson (London, 1876)

Goodridge, John, *John Clare and Community* (Cambridge: Cambridge University Press, 2013)

Grainger, Margaret, *A Descriptive Catalogue of the John Clare Collection in Peterborough Museum and Art Gallery* (Peterborough: Peterborough Museum and Art Gallery, 1973)

Grigson, Geoffrey, *The Englishman's Flora* (London: Phoenix House, 1955)

Hadfield, Miles, *A History of British Gardening*, third edition (London: John Murray, 1979)

Harrap, Anne and Simon, *Orchids of Britain and Ireland*, second edition (London: Bloomsbury, 2009)

Henrey, Blanche, *British Botanical and Horticultural Literature before 1800* (Oxford: Oxford University Press, 1975), three volumes

Heyes, Robert, 'John Clare and Enclosure', *John Clare Society Journal*, 6 (1987), 10–19

— 'Little Hills of Cushioned Thyme', *John Clare Society Journal*, 12 (1993), 32–6

— 'Some friends of John Clare: The poet and the scientists', *Romanticism*, 2 (1996), 98–109

— 'Looking to Futurity': John Clare and Provincial Culture, unpublished Ph.D. thesis, Birkbeck College, University of London, 1999

Hill, Sir John, *The Family Herbal* (Bungay, 1812)

Hobhouse, Penelope, *Plants in Garden History* (London: Pavilion, 1992)

Holdich, Benjamin, *An Essay on the Weeds of Agriculture, with their Common*

190

and Botanical Names, second edition (London, 1826)

Keegan, Bridget, *British Labouring-Class Nature Poetry, 1730–1837* (Basingstoke: Palgrave, 2008)

[Kent, Elizabeth], *Flora Domestica, or, The Portable Flower Garden* (London, 1823)

Lee, James, *An Introduction to Botany* (London, 1760)

Lines, Rodney, 'John Clare and Herbal Medicine', *John Clare Society Journal*, 5 (1986), 16–21

Loudon, J. C., *An Encyclopaedia of Plants* (London, 1836)

Mabey, Richard, *Beechcombings: The Narratives of Trees* (London: Chatto & Windus, 2007)

— *Weeds: The Story of Outlaw Plants* (London: Profile Books, 2010)

Mabey, Richard, supported by Common Ground, *Flora Britannica* (London: Sinclair-Stevenson, 1996)

McCollin, D., Moore, L. and Sparks, T., 'The Flora of a Cultural Landscape', *Biological Conservation*, 92 (2000), 249–63

Maddock, James, *The Florist's Directory* (London, 1822)

Marren, Peter, *Britain's Rare Flowers* (London: T. & A. D. Poyser, 1999)

Martin, Frederick, *The Life of John Clare*, with an introduction and notes by Eric Robinson and Geoffrey Summerfield (London: Frank Cass, 1964)

Miller, Philip, *The Gardener's and Botanist's Dictionary*, edited by T. Martyn (London, 1807), four volumes

Miller, Philip, *The Gardener's Dictionary*, 5th edition (Dublin, 1741)

Miller, Philip, *The Gardener's Dictionary*, 6th edition, corrected and enlarged (London, 1771)

Mitchell, Alan, *The Trees of Britain and Northern Europe* (London: Collins, 1982)

Morton, John, *The Natural History of Northamptonshire* (London, 1712)

Parkinson, John, *Paradisi in Sole, Paradisus Terrestris* (London, 1629)

Parkinson, John, *Theatrum Botanicum* (London, 1640)

Perring, F. H., 'John Clare and Northamptonshire plant records', *Proceedings of the Botanical Society of the British Isles*, 1 (1955), 482–9

Pitt, William, *General View of the Agriculture of the County of Northampton* (Kettering and Daventry, 1809)

[Powell, David], *Catalogue of the John Clare Collection in the Northampton*

Public Library: with Indexes to the Poems in Manuscript (Northampton: Northampton Public Library, 1964)

Preston, C. D., Pearman, D. A. and Dines, T. D., eds, *New Atlas of the British and Irish Flora* (Oxford: Oxford University Press, 2002)

Prior, R. C. A., *On the Popular Names of British Plants*, third edition (London, 1879)

Rackham, Oliver, *Woodlands* (London: Collins New Naturalist Library, 2006)

Raven, Sarah, *Wild Flowers* (London: Bloomsbury, 2011)

Ray, John, *John Ray's Cambridge Catalogue (1660)*, trans. and ed. by P. H. Oswald and C. D. Preston (London: The Ray Society, 2011)

Rothschild, Miriam, and Marren, Peter, *Rothschild's Reserves: Time and Fragile Nature* (Colchester: Harley Books, 1997)

Salisbury, Sir Edward, *Weeds and Aliens*, second edition (London: Collins New Naturalist Library, 1964)

Smith, Sir James E., *A Compendium of the English Flora* (London, 1829)

Smith, Sir James E., *English Botany: or, Coloured Figures of British Plants* ('Sowerby's English Botany') (London, 1790–1813), 36 volumes

Stace, Clive, *New Flora of the British Isles*, third edition (Cambridge: Cambridge University Press, 2010)

Thornton, R. K. R., 'The Flower and the Book: The Gardens of John Clare', *John Clare Society Journal*, 1 (1982), 31–45

Turner, Dawson, and Dillwyn, Lewis Weston, *The Botanist's Guide through England and Wales* (London, 1805), two volumes

Tusser, Thomas, *Five Hundred Points of Good Husbandry* (London, 1812)

Watts, Kenneth, 'Scots pines and droveways', *Wiltshire Folklore*, 19 (1989), 3–6

Wells, Terry C. E., *The Flora of Huntingdonshire and the Soke of Peterborough* (Huntingdon: Huntingdonshire Fauna and Flora Society and T. C. E. Wells, 2003)

White, Simon, 'Landscape Icons and the Community: A Reading of John Clare's "Langley Bush"', *John Clare Society Journal*, 26 (2007), 21–32

Wilkinson, Gerald, *A History of British Trees* (London: Hutchinson, 1981)

Wright, Joseph, *The English Dialect Dictionary* (London, 1898–1905), six volumes

Index of Poems

Poems by Clare referred to in *A John Clare Flora* are indexed here under title or first line. As Clare frequently gave the same title to different poems, the first line has been given in brackets in several cases to avoid confusion. As noted elsewhere (p. 14), the spelling of titles has been standardised to allow readers without access to the Oxford English Texts edition of Clare's poems to locate them in other sources. Individual parts of *The Shepherd's Calendar* are listed under that title rather than separately.

Index of Plants

Only plant names are indexed and not Latin or English family names. Scientific names are in italics. English names are in Roman type, in the case of officially accepted species names with initial capitals and with the qualifier following the noun. Names used by Clare and others which differ from the accepted English names are in quotation marks.

Abies spp. 25
Acer campestre 88
Acer pseudoplanatus 87
Achillea filipendulina 147
Achillea millefolium 147
Aconite, Winter 34
Aconitum lycoctonum 34
Aconitum napellus 34
Acorus calamus 159
Adder's-tongue 21
Aesculus hippocastanum 87
Agrimonia eupatoria 61
Agrimony 61
Agrostemma githago 102
Agrostis capillaris 182
Agrostis stolonifera 182
Ajuga reptans 128
Alcea rosea 90
Alder 64, 72
alga, algae 17, 18
Alliaria petiolata 98
Allium cepa 174
Allium porrum 174
'alloe' 173
Alnus glutinosa 64, 72
'Alnus nigra' 63

Aloe, *Aloe vera* 173
Althaea officinalis 90
Amaranthus caudatus 12, 105
Amaryllis belladonna 174
Anacamptis morio 171
Anacamptis pyramidalis 170
Anagallis arvensis 111
anemones, 'anemonie',
   'anenonie' 35, 36
Anemone, Crown 35
Anemone, Wood 35, 96
Anemone, Yellow 35
Anemone coronaria 35
Anemone nemorosa 35
Anemone ranunculoides 35
'Anemonie pulsitilis of botanists'
   36
Angelica 158
Angelica, Wild 157, 158
Angelica sylvestris 157
Anthriscus sylvestris 156
Anthyllis vulneraria 45, 46
Antirrhinums 124
Antirrhinum majus 123
apple(s) 54, 55, 183
Apple, Crab 54, 91

'Dog mercury' 76
'dog roseys' 62
'dog tree' 76
Dog-rose 61, 62, 63, 121
Dog-violet, Common 82
Dog-violet, Early 82
Dogwood 76, 91, 105, 106, 121
'dotterel(s)', 'dottrels' 69, 120,
    154
'double marigolds' 149
'Double Pink Primrose' 109
Downy-rose, Harsh 62
'drooping willow' 79
'drops of gold' (gooseberries)
    41
Dryopteris dilatata 24
Dryopteris filix-mas 23
'duck meat', 'duckweed' 160
Duckweed, Common 160
'dwarf broom' 51
'Dwarf furze' 52
'Dwarf Orchis' 170
'dwarf willow' 79

'ea[r]thern tongue' 21
Eccremocarpus scaber 135
'eggs-and-bacon' 47
Elder 150, 151
Elder, Dwarf 150, 151
'eldern', 'eldern tree' 53, 120,
    150
elm(s), elm tree 64, 72, 88, 120
Elm, English 64
Elm, Wych 64
Elytrigia repens 184
Enchanter's-nightshade 86

'endive' 141
Epilobium hirsutum 85
Epimedium alpinum 32
Epipactis helleborine 165
Epipactis palustris 165
Equisetum palustre 21
Eranthis hyemalis 34
Erica tetralix 112
Erophila verna 12, 96
Erysimum cheiri 94
Euonymus europaeus 76
Euphorbia lathyris 77
Euphrasia curta 133
Euphrasia nemorosa 133
Evening-primrose, Common 85
'evening primrose' 85
'Evergreen Rose' 63
'everlasting pea' 47, 48
Everlasting-pea, Broad-leaved 48
Everlasting-pea, Narrow-leaved
    48
'everlastings' 147
Eyebright, Common, 133
'eye brights' 133

Fagus sylvatica 67
Fat-hen 12
'Feather Hyacinth' 177
Felwort 114
'Female or Meadow' (orchis) 171
'Fen Orchis' 165
Fennel 129, 156, 157
fern(s) 17, 20, 21, 22, 23, 24, 40,
    73, 112, 147, 181
fern, Broad Buckler- 24
Fern, Marsh 23